CAN YOU HEAR
THE HEARTBEAT?

CAN YOU HEAR
THE HEARTBEAT?

Dave Andrews
with David Engwicht

HODDER & STOUGHTON
LONDON   SYDNEY   AUCKLAND   TORONTO

British Library Cataloguing in Publication Data

Andrews, Dave
    Can you hear the heartbeat?
    1. India (Republic). Christian missions. Australian
    missionaries – Biographies
    I. Title
    266′.0092′4

    ISBN 0 340 51063 3

For Ange

ACKNOWLEDGMENTS

I would like to express my gratitude to my wife, Ange, and my children Evonne and Navdita, who, together with me, have sought to work out our faith in Christ in relation to our life in the community.

Both Ange and I are grateful to our parents, Frank and Margaret Andrews and Jim and Athena Bellas, for the role models they provided for us; to our friends in Dilaram and Aashiana who made our dreams come true against all the odds; and to the people in the Department of Community Services of the Baptist Union of Queensland, and the West End Waiters Union under whose auspices and with whose support this volume has been written.

I am also grateful to David Engwicht, with whom I wrote this material innumerable times and without whose help it would have been unreadable; Di Butterworth, Barbara Day, Trish Hopkinson, Kay Thompson, Audrey Thomson and Wendy van Doore who worked on the book tirelessly to bring it to the light of day; Adrian Reith, who acted as my agent; Juliet Newport, my editor; and Hodder & Stoughton for publishing the book.

In conclusion I gladly acknowledge how much I have gained from the literature which is included in the list of suggestions for study.

Dave Andrews

CONTENTS

A HEART FOR BRINGING GROWTH AND CHANGE

EPILOGUE

INTRODUCING DAVE ANDREWS

It is no accident that you have never heard of Dave Andrews. He's not well known. He'd rather keep it that way.

This book was prised out of a guy who knows that it is easier to *write* about helping others than actually to do it. Dave was persuaded to write this handbook to help ordinary people, such as you and me, live in a way that most people say is impossible.

It isn't. And to prove it, Dave uses his experience and the experiences of his family and friends to show we can do justice to the disadvantaged, just as Jesus did.

This is not an autobiography. That would be a different book; the book that revealed that Dave Andrews is no saint; he does not wear a hair shirt – more likely a T-shirt. It would be a book that would give you a glimpse of Dave at a neighbour's party, laughing uproariously, or getting carried away in a game of tennis or football, or of not being taken seriously by those in authority because he doesn't put on airs, stand on his dignity or wear a suit and tie.

Dave does not take himself seriously – that's important to know because, as you'll discover, Dave takes the subject of this book so seriously you might be forgiven for writing him off as a complete fanatic. But he's not.

Dave and his wife Ange arrived to work in Afghanistan in 1973. At the age of 22, they set up an open home in Delhi – a half-way house for the thousands of disillusioned travellers passing through India.

Within a short time the house was home to scores of junkies, freaks and just plain ordinary people. Some were desperately sick with hepatitis, tuberculosis and typhoid.

Others had been robbed of passports and money. Others were strung out on drugs or disorientated by weird religious experiences. Others felt abandoned in a strange land, far from home.

This community house, with its atmosphere of faith and love, became home for hundreds of people.

For five years Dave and Ange worked intimately with these people, supporting them through their personal crises – even when they hurled plates of food at the wall, stabbed themselves, jumped off the roof, swung on the power lines or ran down the street naked.

Many of these people seemed to remain the same – in spite of the constant care. But others, like Gerhard, experienced dramatic change. Gerhard had grown up wild on the streets of Austria. After some years he became a morphine addict. He skipped military duty, forged his passport and went to India where he overstayed his visa. While staying with Dave and Ange, he became a follower of Jesus.

Gerhard decided to deal with his past and start afresh. He turned himself in to the authorities and served a jail sentence for overstaying his visa. He was then deported to Austria where he served another jail sentence for forging his passport. Because of his pacifist beliefs, Gerhard refused to serve the balance of his military duty and opted to sweep the streets for two years instead. Today, Gerhard is minister of a church in Austria.

Five years after establishing that Dilaram community in India, the number of local people coming for help began to increase. More and more, Dave and Ange became convinced that they should start a community with Indians – solely for Indians.

So began Aashiana, meaning 'nest' – a place where broken people could become whole persons and 'learn to fly again'.

Under the auspices of Aashiana, Dave and Ange and their Indian friends set up a small but unique therapeutic community known as Sahara. Today Sahara is so well regarded as a rehabilitation centre, that people with personality disorders and drug dependency come to it from all over India.

All those who come for help are encouraged to help others. They are put to work serving the poor. Consequently, out of Sahara has emerged Sharan, a community development ministry. Today Sharan is recognised as one of the largest and most energetic voluntary organisations working in the slums and resettlement areas of Delhi, sponsoring educational, health, employment and community programmes with up to 40,000 forgotten people.

In 1984 Dave and Ange had to leave their beloved India when the Indian Government refused to renew their visas to stay.

Back in Australia, they began working with the dispossessed people in that society: Aborigines, refugees, migrants, battered women, broken men, abused children, and those with mental and emotional problems.

They found the principles for working with people who had been pushed to one side were the same in Australia as they were in India.

Before you read this book, there is one other thing you need to know about Dave Andrews. He is dangerous.

For example, after Indira Gandhi was shot, two or three thousand people were killed in twenty-four hours in the riots that followed. Mobs rampaged through streets looking for Sikhs to murder. Dave convinced Tony, another member of the community, that it was their job to go out and save these Sikhs. Finding a besieged house, they put themselves between an armed mob and a Sikh family and saved them from certain death.

Tony remembers that day well: 'I was quite happy to stay in safety behind locked doors until Dave said, "What if it were your family they were murdering?"'

That's why Dave Andrews is dangerous. He is ordinary, yet believes ordinary people should take extraordinary risks to confront the cruelty in our world.

Do you still want to read this book?

David Engwicht
Brisbane, Australia, February 1989

PROLOGUE

HEART TO HEART

At the heart of humanity lies hope. A hope that is as necessary for our survival as earth, air and water.

And at the heart of all hope is a dream – a dream that something, somewhere, sometime will change.

I have a dream.

I dream of a world in which all the resources of the earth will be shared equally between all the people of the earth so that even the most disadvantaged among us will be able to meet their most basic needs with dignity and joy.

I dream of a great society of small communities inter-dependently co-operating to practise political, socio-economic, cultural and personal righteousness and peace.

I dream of vibrant neighbourhoods where people relate to each other as neighbours.

I dream of people developing networks of friendship in which the private pain they carry deep down is allowed to surface and is shared openly in an atmosphere of mutual acceptance and respect.

I dream of people understanding the difficulties they have in common, discerning the problems, discovering solutions, and working together in a spirit of co-operation for personal growth and social change according to the visionary agenda of Jesus of Nazareth.

I dream of every church in every locality acting as a catalyst to make this vision of a renewed world a reality.

Maybe you share some of my dream. It is a dream many of us live for and not a few of us would die for.

If you can hear the heartbeat of such a dream throbbing as hope in your own heart, then this book was written especially for you.

Can You Hear The Heartbeat? will show you the way Jesus transformed his dreams into flesh and blood reality and show you how you can do the same.

There is nothing in this book I did not beg or borrow, if not steal, from others including my wife, my parents, my children, my brothers and sisters, my friends and my fellow workers. Yet everything given by others, I have taken and made my own. Indeed, *Can You Hear The Heartbeat?* is made up of anecdotes from my own involvement in the community which indicates the kind of actions that all of us can take to make our dreams come true for our locality, and ultimately for our world.

Dave Andrews

THE HEART OF LOCAL COMMUNITY INVOLVEMENT

1

SCANDALOUS LOVE

How did Jesus relate to people in the community?

Simon paced uneasily up and down the verandah waiting for the first guests to arrive at his dinner party. He had spent all his life climbing the social ladder. This was his big opportunity to impress and make sure he climbed one more rung. After all, it wasn't just anybody who could promise such a prize guest of honour as Jesus from Nazareth.

The dinner got off to a flying start. This Jesus character seemed to have the knack of breaking the ice with the upper-class guests. They laughed at his jokes and were enthralled with his yarns. As the entrée dishes were being collected by the servants, Simon listened to the animated chatter that filled the room – and inwardly smiled. People were enjoying themselves.

But suddenly the chatter and hilarity died. Wondering what on earth could have gone wrong, Simon looked up, and to his amazement, standing in the doorway was the local prostitute.

Her heavy perfume filled the room. Nervously the dignitaries turned back to the plates of food – in silence. For some, her very presence inflamed feelings of shame and guilt. Others tried not to leer at her low-cut dress too long.

Slowly the prostitute made her way to the head of the table where the guest of honour reclined.

Now this lady of the night began to create a real scene by sobbing uncontrollably. Hot tears streamed through her heavy make up and fell on Jesus's feet.

The guests almost choked with embarrassment as the prostitute took her hair and began wiping the tears from Jesus's dusty feet.

What happened next was a scene that none of those guests would ever forget – a scene made all the more pungent by the customs of the day. For men to speak to women in public was forbidden. To touch was completely taboo.

As if in total privacy, the prostitute enacted a strange ritual of love. Taking an expensive jar of perfumed cream, she massaged it into Jesus's feet. Jesus, taking her hand, looked deep into her eyes and said, 'Thanks for showing your love for me so beautifully. I accept you just as you are, even if others don't. Go in peace.' (Story found in Luke 7:36–50, adapted.)

It is impossible to overestimate the profound effect Jesus had on the common people. In fact Jesus was a favoured guest at parties thrown by people all over town.

What was it about Jesus that made the prostitute feel so comfortable in his presence that she could enter a stranger's house, break all accepted social customs and express her inner feelings for him in such an intimate fashion?

These people felt an irresistible attraction to Jesus because in him they found total acceptance – unconditional and non-condemnatory. It was an acceptance that was neither patronising nor manipulative. Instead it was characterised by a profound respect for the person that powerfully transformed lack of self-esteem into courageous self-respect.

Jesus created a refuge within himself where outcasts felt safe to rip away their masks and expose the secret turmoil of their souls.

Those who shared their secrets with him found he did not point the finger at their faults, but lent them a hand to deal with their failings and fears.

People loved being around Jesus because they could stop playing games and find genuine acceptance. That acceptance set them free to be fully human and fully alive.

Is it any wonder then that wherever Jesus went he was besieged by people. People were so persistent in clamouring for his attention that he often went days without a meal. Though instinctively repulsed by the arrogant judgmentalism of the Pharisees, the self-righteous religionists of his day, people were instinctively drawn to the gracious, non-judgmental manner of Jesus.

It is amazing the effect offering non-patronising acceptance to others can have. I vividly remember the day Brenda turned up at our house. She was stoned out of her brain. Brenda visited every day for a while – but then suddenly stopped.

My wife Ange went with Brenda's brother who was staying with us to visit her at her home. When they arrived, there was Brenda, sitting on the roof – stoned. In fact she was waiting for a delivery of drugs and had stolen her mother's jewellery to sell in exchange.

After being coaxed down from the roof, Brenda ran to the bathroom, locked the door and slit her wrists. Brenda's brother broke down the door and Ange brought Brenda home. For the next five months Ange spent all day, every day constantly by her side. She helped Brenda start her own small business making stationery.

Brenda became a follower of Jesus and became a volunteer in an organisation working with drug addicts, and eventually married one of the co-ordinators. Today they run a community home for drug addicts.

But practising acceptance is not always so straightforward. It can be rather complicated, as Jesus himself discovered when the prostitute embraced him in public. Ange and I once had a similar experience.

Anne had a notorious sexual history and everyone around town seemed to know every intimate detail. When she would come to visit us she would grab any available guy around and would begin hugging and kissing them uncontrollably. Then she would turn to the audience she had generated through her bizarre behaviour and brag for hours about her sexual adventures.

Both Ange and I wanted to extend unconditional acceptance to Anne, but didn't know how to do it in a way that would discourage her from acting in an overtly sexual way. We eventually evolved a plan that could give her all the affection she needed without encouraging her to flaunt her self. Every time she felt the urge to kiss someone, she would go to Ange and cover her with kisses. This ritual happened at least once a day, every day for six months. In private, Anne would talk through her sexual hassles. In public, we encouraged her to relate to people intimately without getting sexually involved.

We did not condemn her for her sexual behaviour. Instead we communicated to Anne her value as a person. Anne never felt judged. Instead she felt loved, not because of her value as a sex object, but because of her intrinsic value as a human being.

Unconditional acceptance provided a context in which Anne could be transformed. That transformation as yet is neither complete nor permanent. But Anne, who was previously unemployable, has had a job as a well-respected private secretary for a number of years. She now carries an air of dignity as she goes about her work.

How did Jesus relate to people in the community?
Jesus enjoyed a very special relationship with people, especially those on the fringe of society. He treated them with respect and extended to them unconditional, non-condemnatory acceptance.

IDEAS FOR MEDITATION, DISCUSSION AND ACTION

1. **Recall**: Remember a time when you met someone you didn't like. How did you react to them?
2. **Reflect**: Why did Jesus accept those he did not agree with?
3. **Relate**: How do we react to the way Jesus related to people?

2

RELENTLESS TENDERNESS

How did Jesus understand his role in the community?

One balmy Sabbath, Jesus visited the Synagogue in Nazareth and was asked to take the scripture reading. Turning to Isaiah he read:

> 'The Spirit of God has got hold of me,
> and is urging me to do a special job;
> share good news with the poor;
> free the prisoners;
> help the handicapped;
> and smash the shackles of the oppressed . . .'
>
> (Luke 4:18–19, adapted)

Jesus made this statement the mandate for his life's work.

Essential to Jesus's understanding of his role in the community was the Spirit of God. He claimed that the Spirit of God, the essential character of God, had penetrated every fibre of his being. He made time and space for the Spirit. Even in the midst of a pressing schedule he would take time out to go into the mountains to pray, like a son laying his head on his Father's heart to hear his heartbeat. After these sessions in solitude he could say, 'I and my Father are one.' What motivated God, motivated him – he was God incarnate.

The Spirit of God set the agenda for his involvement in

society. It inspired the creative, yet controversial actions he took, and gave him courage to carry them through.

And what was the concern of the Spirit?

The plight of the poor. People who, though sinners, were also victims of other people's sins – victims of greed and injustice.

The predicament of the prisoners and the handicapped. People locked out of all meaningful participation by bars of steel and stigma. People in whom all hope had been crushed; who felt consigned forever to long days and longer nights of quiet desperation and absolute despair.

What was the commitment of the Spirit to the people who were the subjects of his concern?

To motivate someone to share the good news that these forgotten people had not been forgotten by God or God's people. And to share that good news by being prepared to struggle in solidarity with them for their release from all that would debilitate them as human beings – setting them free to be fully human and fully alive. In so doing, these bearers of good news would become a living memory of God's love for the underdog.

Jesus took the Spirit of God to heart. He made the concerns and commitment of the Spirit his own. He became a person who was forgetful of himself, yet lived in constant remembrance of those in the community who were in distress. He used all of his time, energy and resources to address their distress. He struggled with them for their liberty.

Jesus did not view his role in the community as a religious rite or as social work. It was essentially a spiritual struggle for total liberation, culminating in his ultimate self-sacrifice and his resurrection.

Being a follower of Jesus is not a matter of subscribing to certain dogma, obeying laws, or getting others to subordinate themselves to them. The essence of being a follower of Jesus is to live in sympathy with God as Jesus did; feeling the throb of God's heartbeat, to know what causes him pleasure and what causes him pain. To struggle to please him and diminish his pain.

What pleases God? Wherever love is a way of life and justice is done for the welfare of all.

And what pains God? The suffering of the oppressed. In fact, the heart of the powerless is so much a part of God's heart that when the knife of oppression pierces their heart . . . it pierces his heart also.

Both Ange and I learnt from our parents what it means to live in sympathy with God's heart for people.

My mother and father, Frank and Margaret Andrews, not only took people into their hearts – but also into their home. Home was always open for those in distress. People going through difficult times would stay for a day, a year, or however long they needed.

As a young impressionable boy I can remember the excitement that some of those people brought to our house. For example, the cat burglar who had just got out of jail and showed us how easy it was to break into our house. We never bothered locking the house after that!

Not all encounters were exciting. Having a man who had stabbed someone to death sleep in the room next to me made for some very uneasy nights. But my parents taught me to relate to these people as people – not as some subhuman species with tags like 'thieves' and 'murderers'.

Ange's parents, James and Athena Bellas, operated the Star Milk Bar in downtown Brisbane, famous all over town for its quality food and drinks.

Every morning, very early, my father-in-law would open up the café. When he did, it seemed like all the hobos would emerge from the hiding places they had huddled in during the night. He would welcome them in; sit them down; serve them tea, coffee and toast; and chat with them about the night they had just had and the day ahead.

If anyone needed a job he would leave his brothers in charge of the café and go job hunting with them. If they got in trouble with the police, he would visit them in jail. He regularly visited those in hospital. When friendless people died, he would go to their funerals, even if he was the only one there.

Ange's dad would invite folk home to share a meal with the family – even though the Bellases had eight children of their own. Meals at the Bellases were even more famous than those at the Star Milk Bar so there was never a shortage of guests!

So Ange grew up in a large family that was always being enlarged to make room for others. Her parents enabled Ange to understand the commitment of the Spirit to people in need.

Both Frank and Margaret Andrews and James and Athena Bellas have been shining examples of those who are not preoccupied with themselves. As they made time and space for God, they began to make time and space for the people God was passionately concerned about. They took these people into their hearts and their homes. They became good news for people going through bad times.

How did Jesus understand his role in the community?
His role was to live in sympathy with the Spirit – to feel the heartbeat of God. He felt the pain of God when people suffered and he struggled to diminish that pain.

IDEAS FOR MEDITATION, DISCUSSION
AND ACTION

1. **Recall**: Remember a time when your heart was moved by the plight of someone in need. How did you feel?
2. **Reflect**: How do you think Jesus would have felt?
3. **Relate**: How can we become more sensitive to the pain of others?

3

VULGAR INVOLVEMENT

How did Jesus go about his work in the community?

It is one thing to feel empathy with the poor – quite another actually to get involved.

How can **we** be involved?

Relating to others comes naturally to some people; but not to all of us – certainly not to me. Many of us feel awkward around people, especially those on the fringe of society. Many of us think we don't have the qualifications or skills to deal with these kinds of people.

So when we think of working with disadvantaged people in the community, we think of training as an expert, or employing one. The rationale is clear. People need professional help. We simply don't have the expertise to be involved. Helping others is clearly a job for the experts.

But Jesus had little time for experts.

Jesus never trained in the Rabbinic schools, nor was he ever ordained as a Rabbi, a minister of religion.

Nor was he a doctor, lawyer or social worker. He was a carpenter . . . just one of the gang.

Not only did Jesus not have professional welfare expertise – he constantly attacked the arrogant authority that the experts abrogated to themselves. Why?

Not because the expertise of experts was of no value. But because Jesus knew most experts were using their expertise as a means of exploiting the very people they were meant to help.

Things haven't changed much. Many welfare organisations, religious and secular, can be fronts for exploitation of the poor. In fact, such institutions have a vested interest in keeping the poor poor, that is, dependent on the services of the organisation for their survival. That way the organisation can survive.

When was the last time you heard of a welfare organisation closing its doors because it had so empowered those it sought to help that the organisation became redundant? Is it any wonder then that Jesus rejected employing experts as the way of bringing liberation to the oppressed?

Instead he chose a radically different alternative. The amazing thing about this alternative is that when uneducated, unqualified and apparently totally inept people follow his approach, they often have a far more dramatic effect on a community than a whole army of experts.

The approach advocated by Jesus was one of vulgar involvement. Paul explains this approach, 'Though Jesus was equal with God, he did not count equality with God a thing to be hung up on or held on to. Instead, he emptied himself, taking the form of a servant. He was born in the likeness of ordinary people and being found in human form he humbled himself and became obedient even unto death.' (Philippians 2:6–8)

1. Christ gave up the security, status and privilege of position to get involved in the community. That meant accepting discomfort.
2. He emptied himself of his own concerns, immersed himself in the lives of other people and allowed their concerns to fill his life.
3. He did not try to be different from the people around him, but lived like an ordinary person; dressing the same way; speaking the same earthy language; and experiencing the same hassles and hardship as everybody else.
4. He became a servant in the midst of those struggles, seeking to bring change and growth that would set people free to live life to the full.

5. Jesus was prepared to pay the price for his involvement with people in blood, sweat and tears.

If we are going to have the same dramatic impact that Jesus had on his community, then we must follow his example of involvement. We cannot do it vicariously through others. We must get involved ourselves.

Yes, there is a role for organisations. They may provide a useful framework for the work we want to do in the community. And there is a role for professionals. They may provide extra insight that is useful for increasing the effectiveness of the work we want to do.

But there is simply no substitute for hands-on involvement. If the job is to be done, we must get our hands dirty. Getting our hands dirty means going about our work the same way Jesus did.

1. We must be willing to set aside our concerns for security and status. We must be willing to forgo the comforts that privilege and position bring in order to meet the disadvantaged on their territory and on their terms.

2. We must empty ourselves of our preoccupation with our own thoughts and feelings so that we can immerse ourselves in the lives of others and allow their thoughts and feelings, joys and anguish to fill us.

3. We must not try to be different from the people around us, but instead discover the similarities in our common humanity. We all get sick. We all get tired. We all grow old. We all die. We can share these common troubles with our brothers and sisters in the community – even if our beliefs are poles apart.

4. We must enter into people's struggles with them, and in the context of the struggle, serve them as a servant. Our relationships in the community should be marked by an uncommon care; a quality of life that reflects the love of God.

5. We must be willing to pay the price of bringing life to people in our community. That price is a painful dying

to ourselves in the midst of frustrations, tensions and difficulties.

Unfortunately, there are no easy options. If there were, I'm sure Jesus would have known about them and taken them. Instead, there is just one hard option – the vulgarity of risking all the hassles, heartaches and headaches of becoming involved with people for the sake of love and justice.

For many of us, this may seem like an unrealistic ideal, achievable only by saints and not mere mortals like you and me. Well, it is an ideal but certainly not unrealistic. I have met many less than perfect individuals who live out this ideal in a less than perfect world.

Freda is one such woman. Freda is a medical practitioner. She could earn a big income, drive a big car, live in a big house and enjoy the prestige and kudos of being a doctor. But she doesn't. She has rejected the prestige that comes with being a doctor. Most people don't even know she is a doctor, they just relate to her as Freda.

Freda rides a bike around the neighbourhood and greets strangers in the street. She is not full of herself and her own opinions. She gives other people space to be themselves and have their say.

She works for Aboriginal health, but not as the outside expert who commutes from a middle class suburb. Freda lives where they live and fights the battles they fight. She takes to the streets with them to protest at injustice and cops the same abuse they get. She gives most of her substantial income away and lives on a meagre allowance so she can identify more closely with those she seeks to help.

Freda understands the difference between service and servanthood. Acts of service are those acts we decide to do in our efforts to help others. Acts of servanthood are those acts others decide they would like us to do for them. She has felt the heartbeat of God for her community and responded by giving herself as a servant to those she seeks to help.

Freda is having a quiet, but significant impact on her community. So can we.

How did Jesus go about his work in the community?
He did not set himself up as an expert, but simply gave himself as a servant to those he sought to help.

IDEAS FOR MEDITATION, DISCUSSION AND ACTION

1. **Recall:** Remember a time when you lent someone a helping hand. How did you go about it?
2. **Reflect:** How do you imagine Jesus might have gone about it?
3. **Relate:** How similar are the ways we go about our work?

4

JUST VALUES

What values did Jesus use in his work in the community?

The stories that Jesus told revealed the values that guided his work in the community. None reveal his preoccupation with justice more than the parable called 'The Last Judgement'.

At the end of time, Jesus said, the True Leader will gather everyone together for the final reckoning. Like a stockman culling wild horses, the True Leader will divide those gathered into two groups. Those who have done the right thing will be put on his right and those who haven't on his left.

To those on his right, the True Leader issues an invitation to a never-ending party. 'Come!' he says, 'For I was hungry as a horse and you gave me a feed. I was as dry as a parched gully and you gave me a drink. I just arrived in town and you took me into your home. My clothes were in tatters and you gave me a great outfit. I was sick in bed and you came and spent time with me. I was stuck in jail and you stuck by me and my family.'

The people on the right were stunned. 'When on earth did we see you hungry and give you a feed or thirsty and give you a drink?' they queried. 'When did we meet you after you had just arrived in town and give you a bed for the night? When were you sick in bed and we visited you? When were you stuck in jail and we looked after you and your family?'

The True Leader replied, 'Whenever you did the right

thing by those who most people couldn't give a damn for, you did the right thing by me.'

Then turning to those on his left the True Leader says, 'Get out. You're in big trouble! You can go to hell with all those who made life a misery for others. I was hungry and you never gave me a feed, thirsty and you never gave me a drink, lonely without a friend and you walked by, half-naked and you didn't give me clothes, sick in bed and stuck in jail and you didn't even visit.'

Those on the left were bewildered. 'When did we see you hungry or thirsty?' they cried. 'When did we see you lonely without a friend or half-naked and badly in need of a new set of clothes? When did we see you sick in bed or stuck in jail?'

The True Leader replied, 'Whenever you ignored the needs of those whom most people consider least, you ignored me.' (Matthew 25:31–46, adapted)

The shock for the religious leaders of Jesus's day (and for most of us today) is that Jesus insisted that people will not be judged on whether they have subscribed to the right set of doctrines, followed the right code of behaviour, or served the church organisation well. Their acceptability to God will be judged solely on how they have treated those considered least.*

This then gives us the clue as to the values that guided Jesus's work in the community. **He gave most consideration to those usually considered least**. He argued that all work in the community should be judged on the basis of how it affected those usually considered least.

---

*There are some Christians who argue that this principle only applies to their treatment of fellow Christians – not everyone in their neighbourhood. Such an interpretation is a denial of the very spirit of this story. It should be noted that those we are required to do good to are defined, not in relationship to Christ or the church, but simply in terms of their needs. It is to 'the hungry, the thirsty, the naked, the sick and the imprisoned' that we are to respond. The fact that the True Leader refers to these needy as 'brethren' is only a further indication of how strongly he feels kinship with the needy.

To put the principle of giving priority to those considered least into practice involves three phases:

1. Search out those considered least.
2. Treat those considered least as those we consider most.
3. Do something practical to help them.

Each of us is located in various communities. Communities of religion, residence, work, culture and interest. As we move around these communities we can put this principle into operation by following these three simple steps.

1. SEARCH OUT THOSE CONSIDERED LEAST

This may seem very simple, but can be very difficult. Those considered least are often very hard to find because by their very definition, they are the people we usually ignore.

We ignore them because we simply don't see them. Women, battered quietly behind closed doors. Men, locked away behind prison walls. The elderly, shut away in their homes year after year. Those with handicaps, excluded from our workplaces, churches and shopping centres.

Alternatively, we see them, but ignore them because we don't see them as people. Instead we label them as old codgers, young punks, junkies, winos, derelicts, bludgers, bums, fags, pimps, whores, schizos, crims, crazies, wogs, dagos and boongs. Once they are labelled we don't have to deal with them as people who have the same longing for love as we have.

Then there are the people we see as people but whose pain we don't see. The neighbour we wave to every day but whose anguish we know nothing about. The relative who cries in the privacy of their own room. The fellow parishioner who smiles sweetly, shakes our hand, and goes home to a living hell.

So how on earth do we find those in need if the people and their pain are hidden? By going out of our way to search for them. This involves looking with eyes that are no longer blinded by bias in the places where these people are hidden; not only in prisons, hospitals, nursing homes, boarding houses, sheltered workshops, rehabilitation centres, and alley ways, but also in our own back yard, in our office or our factory.

And we find the pain that is hidden by establishing friendships of mutual acceptance in which people feel secure enough to uncover their suffering and confide the reality of their struggles.

2. TREAT THOSE WE CONSIDER LEAST AS THOSE WE CONSIDER MOST

This will involve a radical reorientation of our lives. Normally we put ourselves first and others last. After all, that's conventional wisdom.

Where we are concerned for others we put the strong, the intelligent, the witty, the attractive and the rich first and the weak, the simple, the ordinary, the plain and the poor last. After all, if we put ourselves out for others, we want to relate to those who will return our investment in them with dividends.

Where we are concerned for the weak, the simple, the ordinary, the plain and the poor, we put those with most potential for improvement first and those with least potential last. After all, if we are going to go out of our way to help somebody, who wants to put effort into someone who will not reward us by becoming a success story?

Putting the last first means becoming committed to the principle that we cannot do justice in our community unless we put those at the bottom of the heap at the top of our priorities.

We must make conscious decisions to fly in the face of conventional wisdom, invest ourselves in people who

cannot repay us and willingly associate ourselves with
ventures that will fail.

On a day to day basis it will mean making individual,
family and community decisions to allocate time, energy,
money and all the resources at our disposal so as to do
justice to those usually considered least.

3. DO SOMETHING PRACTICAL TO
   HELP THEM

In the story of the Last Judgment, Jesus suggested the way
to do the right thing by those usually considered least was
simply to meet their needs. In Jesus's mind, there was no
doubt that we all have the capacity to meet the basic needs
of our neighbours. We can all give a cup of water, invite
someone for a meal, befriend someone who is lonely, take
someone into our home or help someone out who has
hassles.

He didn't tell us to psychoanalyse the poor or set up big
welfare agencies for the marginalised. Instead he told us to
share our resources – even if all we have at our disposal is a
cup of tea and a slice of bread.

The problem most of us have with this response is that
giving someone a drink or a feed doesn't seem to deal with
the structural causes of poverty and seems a totally in-
adequate response. It is too simplistic. How can sharing
a meal with someone solve the structural problems of
poverty?

However Jesus insists that if all of us shared our resources, then the structural problems of poverty would be
solved. Sharing our resources undermines the foundations
of institutionalised greed and the consequent inequality.

Our willingness gladly to share ourselves and our possessions with anyone in need, may not solve all the problems in the world. But it may meet the needs of one person,
and in so doing, show that sharing is the way that all the
problems of world poverty could be solved.

We can all do something practical to help people in need. But we need to recognise that not all help is helpful. In fact, some help can do more harm than good. Sometimes we are not addressing the real need. We make assumptions about what is wrong. And we make assumptions about how to put it right. In fact we may be missing the point completely. Just because we feel good about what we are doing doesn't necessarily mean we are doing anyone any good.

But even if we do address a real need, our method of helping may not be helpful. We may be supercilious and patronising. Even if we give them a meal, our attitudes may make them sick. We may invite them into our house, but they may not feel at home.

Help is only helpful if it meets a need in such a way that it builds a person up and doesn't put anyone down in the process. The issue is not whether we feel good about what we are doing, but whether what we do and how we do it does any good for those in need.

The three steps involved in putting the last first is illustrated best by a couple who live in our neighbourhood.

When Kevin and Rona moved into our neighbourhood they began a search for those avoided by others.

In their street they found a family where the father had molested his daughter. The rest of the community had withdrawn in horror.

Down the road they found a row of boarding houses in which people labelled as 'derros' stayed. These people, disowned by family and society, seldom had visitors.

Under a bridge they found a bunch of people, labelled by society as 'hobos'. At night these people would sleep at a hostel nearby.

On walls in the area they found racist graffiti which said, 'Asians Go Home!'

Having found those in their neighbourhood who were usually put last, Kevin and Rona took the second step and **made these people their priority**. They arranged their lives so both of them needed only to work part time so they could both devote time to serving these people.

Having made these people their priority they took the third step and **did something practical to help them**.

They stood by the family isolated by the scandal of child abuse and offered them practical support.

They took regular walks past the boarding houses and greeted those who sat on the verandahs, eventually forming a friendship with one of the men.

Along with some friends, they helped check the people from under the bridge into the hostel and helped serve the evening meal.

They helped make the victims of the racist graffiti feel at home by becoming involved in a migrant and refugee support group which gives English language and Australian culture encounters to the Asians in their own homes.

Kevin and Rona have proved that putting the last first is possible and that ordinary people can meet needs through simple, unpretentious acts of service.

What values did Jesus use in his work in the community? He gave priority to those considered least. He sought them out, treated them as if they were the most important people in the world and did something practical to help them.

IDEAS FOR MEDITATION, DISCUSSION AND ACTION

1. **Recall**: Who are the people in your community considered least?

2. **Reflect**: How do we imagine Jesus would want us to relate to these people?

3. **Relate**: What would it mean for us if we made those considered least our most important priority?

5

GOOD STRATEGIES

What strategies did Jesus use in his work in the community?

Jesus's aim was the spiritual transformation of every facet of society. He used a variety of methods to bring about this transformation.

The following are five different kinds of strategies Jesus used to address the financial disadvantage of the poor. But these same methods were used to transform all aspects of society: religious, cultural, political, social and economic.

1. EMERGENCY RELIEF

Jesus took it upon himself physically to meet the need. The classic example was his decision to provide food for 5,000 hungry people who were desperately weak because they had not eaten for three days. (Mark 6:37–44)

Jesus and his disciples also gave regular gifts of money to the poor so their immediate needs could be met. (John 12:4–6 & 13:29)

2. FORMATIVE EDUCATION

Jesus also taught the community to meet its own needs. Jesus taught Zacchaeus that all the needs of society could be met if all shared. As a result Zacchaeus was inspired to redistribute his riches to the poor and to make restitution for his bribery and robbery. (Luke 19)

The teaching of Jesus, epitomised in the Sermon on the Mount, promoted attitudes to life that would create a more just society. 'Give to anyone who asks for anything . . . Lend . . . without expecting anything back.' (Luke 6:30, 35) 'Do not be anxious about your life, about what you can get to eat and drink.' (Matthew 6:25) 'Set your heart on God's movement and his justice . . .' (Matthew 6:33)

3. DIRECT ACTION

Jesus often confronted those who oppressed the poor – but were unwilling to change their ways voluntarily. The best known of these direct action confrontations was his non-violent attack on the temple. (Luke 19)

The people he challenged in this confrontation were not only the religious and political establishment, but also the economic establishment: the bankers, the stockbrokers, businessmen and merchants. Under the corrupt rule of Annas and Caiaphas the high priests (who also exercised political rulership under the Romans) these men had amassed huge wealth at the expense of the poor.

4. MODEL FORMATION

Jesus modelled alternative methods of structuring economic relationships which did justice to the poor. For example, Jesus and his large band of at last seventy followers shared a common purse. Expenses were met out of this common fund and the excess shared with the poor. (John 12)

5. COMMUNITY DEVELOPMENT

Jesus encouraged a movement of people who would develop the principles, practices and procedures he had modelled with his disciples. The early church became that movement. They continued the practice of commonality; determined not to see their money or possessions as their own but as belonging to those who had less than themselves. The result? One witness claimed that there was not a single person in their community left in need. (Acts 2:43–47 & 4:32–37)

Let me give you one example of each of these strategies from our own experience to show how they may be employed in your neighbourhood.

Emergency relief. Nick and Sandra, who live around the corner from us, regularly share nutritious meals with neighbours who live on the breadline. They have also taken in a refugee, Paulie. Paulie in turn is supporting four refugee families that he and his friends have helped settle into the neighbourhood.

Formative education. Daryl and Frances had considered getting involved in the community, but they remained pre-occupied with their own private world – that is until Daryl found himself dying in hospital with a brain tumour. He recalled conversations with Ange and me, about the last Judgment, which he had not acted on. He decided that if he survived he would only work part time and the rest of time in their community. Today Daryl and Frances are helping homeless people in our community.

Direct action. The 1987 Australian Federal election campaign degenerated into an attempt to buy votes by each party trying to outdo each other with the size of their promised tax cuts. This unabashed appeal to greed at the expense of the blatant needs in our community disturbed me and a number of my friends.

To draw attention to the greed that our politicians were openly promoting, we decided to give away $1000 in $2 notes in the shopping mall in the middle of Brisbane, the sacred centre of consumerism of our city. Wearing T-shirts with the slogan 'Greed Destroys' we gave the money to a lunch-time crowd, and almost created a riot as the crowd became possessed by their own greed and fought over the

money. The riot became a prophetic exposure of the greed
that grips our society. The event made national television
and created numerous opportunities to talk about the greed
that is strangling the poor.

Model formation.   Ange and I try to model our beliefs in
our own family life. We specifically try to practise simplicity, solidarity and service.

We have chosen to live on the poverty line and to give
away everything we earn above that amount. We have
adjusted our standard of living to do this, living in the
cheapest house we could get and driving a car (if it can be
called a car) which does not require hefty repayments or
expensive insurance.

Our lives are open rather than closed to the struggles of
the people around about us. We've adjusted our style of
living to do this, meeting strangers, visiting the sick
and welcoming all and sundry. Through the years we
have taken hundreds of people into our home and our
hearts.

We live a life of quiet help and loud protest. On the one
hand we try to help people in need in any way we can. On
the other hand, now and again, we protest publicly against
ways that people we are working with are disadvantaged by
our society.

Community development.   A few of us in our area have
formed a 'Waiters' Union'. Together we seek to develop a
network of people in the community who will be committed
to wait on God and their neighbours, attending to their
agendas.

Among other things, the 'Waiters' Union' provides a
community meal for up to sixty people every fortnight.
Those who are estranged from society are glad to get
together for a special meal. But we try not only to give these
people food, but also to give them friendship. In the
context of the meal we talk with them about their needs and
try to find ways to meet them.

There is always a big debate as to which of these five
strategies for community involvement is the most effective.

For instance, we were caught in the midst of the housing crisis caused by World Expo 88 which was held in our area. Hundreds of low-income families were made homeless as landlords jacked up rents to cash in on the influx of visitors or sold their properties for redevelopment. Some groups argued for relief; an injection of funds to provide additional welfare accommodation. Others argued for education; a presentation of the facts and figures in the media to stir the conscience of the community. Still others argued for action; an intervention by squatting in accommodation needed by low-income people who were being dispossessed.

Certain groups of people seem to favour one kind of response no matter what the problem. For example, charitable groups usually opt for relief; religious groups usually opt for relief or education; radical groups usually opt for education or action. Rarely do these groups consider the other options available.

All five options have their time and place. Whenever we are confronted with a community problem we must choose which of the options is most appropriate for that particular case. It may be that a number of the options must be adopted.

If all the options are crucial as strategies for transformation, we must ask ourselves why we tend to avoid certain strategies. All of us are predisposed towards certain types of strategies because of our personalities – yet I suspect there are often deeper reasons we avoid certain types of strategies.

Some of us avoid emergency relief because we do not want to share our own hard-earned resources to meet other people's immediate needs. We will only be free to opt for emergency relief if we recognise that other people have as much right to our hard-earned cash and possessions as we have.

A few of us avoid formative education because training others to meet their own needs involves a long-term, rather than a short-term commitment. We will only be free to opt for formative education if we are prepared to invest the same time training people in life skills that others have invested in us.

A lot of us avoid direct action because we are afraid of confrontation, preferring the support of the power brokers for our charitable work rather than risking their opposition by exposing their manipulation of the people we are working with. We will only be free to opt for direct action if we join the ranks of those who are willing to suffer at the hands of the power brokers for their stand against institutionalised injustice.

Many of us may avoid model formation because we would prefer to put the onus for change on to others rather than ourselves. We will only be free to opt for model formation if we realise that the only way to change our world is to change our own way of life.

Most of us avoid community development because we want to give people a hand but we are wary about letting things get out of hand, at least out of our hands. We will only be free to opt for community development if we are willing to work hand in hand with others, allowing the community to set the agenda for our involvement.

What strategies did Jesus use in his work in the community? He utilised a variety of strategies including emergency relief, formative education, direct action, model formation and community development. He used the most appropriate strategy for each occasion.

IDEAS FOR MEDITATION, DISCUSSION AND ACTION

1. **Recall**: What is the most crucial issue your community needs to deal with?
2. **Reflect**: What strategies might Jesus suggest be used to deal with the issue?
3. **Relate**: What scenario can we imagine taking place if we implemented these strategies?

6

ESSENTIAL RESOURCES

What resources did Jesus use in his work in the community?

Every time I talk with people about becoming involved with the community, they usually raise one of two questions.

'Where can we get the money for the programme?'
'How can we motivate the number of people we need to do the job?'

Both these reactions reveal what most people consider to be the essential resources for successful community involvement.

Most people believe we can only do significant community work if we have access to a lot of money or a large number of people. But how essential is having a lot of money or a large number of people to doing significant community work?

On two occasions Jesus sent his followers out into various villages to do community work. On the first occasion he forbade them to take any money. (Matthew 10:9) On the second occasion he allowed them to take money. The moral of the story? Money is not a primary, but a secondary resource.

On both these occasions, Jesus sent them out in groups of two. The moral of the story? When two people relate to a third and form a group of three in the community, you have an adequate number of people to begin a significant movement of change in a community. Apparently Jesus considered there was something more important than a lot of money or a large number of people in bringing about change in the community.

Most attempts to bring about change in the community don't come unstuck because the people involved lack money or numbers. Most come unstuck because personality clashes and power struggles cause the groups to self-destruct. The people involved lack the power to change themselves, let alone their society.

The most important factor in bringing about change in our community is the power for us to be able to manage our own affairs in a way that gives everyone a fair go. Power that enables us to transcend our selfishness, resolve our conflicts, and enable us to deal with issues in a way that does justice to everybody involved. Without that power, Jesus maintained, we should not even make a start at working in our communities because we will wind up destroying the very society we are trying to create. (Luke 24:49)

Conversely, Jesus claimed that with that power, nothing could stop us from bringing significant change. Neither the paucity of our own resources. Nor the internal or external forces opposed to us. (Matthew 17:20) Thus, before Jesus sent out his followers to do community work, he imparted to them what he referred to as 'the power of the Spirit' (John 20:21–22).

The Spirit 'is not a spirit of timidity, but of power . . . characterised by discipline of ourselves . . . and compassion for others. (2 Timothy 1:7) So as we open ourselves to the Spirit, the Spirit produces in us the power to control ourselves and the love for others that is necessary to set us free to serve society.

Now most people who have been involved in trying to bring about change in the community would find it easy to accept Jesus's idea that power was the most important factor in the process. But many would find it more difficult to accept the kind of power, the power of the Spirit, that Jesus advocated. Not merely because of the spiritual language Jesus used to describe the power he advocated, but because of the substantial difference between the traditional notion of power to which many of us acquiesce and the alternative notion of power advocated by Jesus.

There are two ways of understanding power.

Traditionally our notion of power has been defined as the ability to control other people. The traditional notion of power emphasises the possibility of bringing about change through coercion – making others change according to our ideas.

As a way of dealing with the disparity between the rich and the poor, the traditional approach has been to mobilise the have-nots to overthrow the haves and share the spoils of victory.

While the traditional definition of power is taking control of our lives by taking control of **others**, Jesus advocated a radical alternative – taking control of our lives by taking control of **ourselves**. This alternative emphasises bringing change by conversion – a conversion that changes us individually and collectively. It breaks the control others have over us, and it rids us of the desire to control others.

The way this alternative view of power would deal with the disparity between the rich and the poor is to encourage everyone, no matter where they are on the have-a-lot have-a-little continuum, to recognise the greed that grips all of us, and to break the power of selfishness over our lives by sharing with others. Those who have much would be encouraged to give much and those who have little would be encouraged to give little. But all would be encouraged to give so that there is enough for all.

The traditional notion of power is popular because it often brings quick, dramatic results. It is also convenient because both the goodies and baddies are easily identified. Those with the vested interest are always others – never ourselves. Those that need to be confronted are always others – never ourselves. Conflict is resolved by eliminating others and elevating ourselves.

But unfortunately the traditional use of power is characterised by short-term gains for some and long-term losses for all. The issue of continued vested interests, the cause of all injustice, is not dealt with. Even those vested interests that are dealt with are not dealt with justly. Every violent revolution, no matter how pure the motives, inevitably betrays those it seeks to liberate.

The alternative notion of power is unpopular because it is usually a slow, undramatic process. It also makes uncomfortable demands upon us. The goodies and baddies are no longer clearly defined in terms of them and us. We all have to face our own inherent badness. We have to confront our own vested interests. We have to affirm the inherent goodness even in our enemies. Conflicts have to be resolved in a way that eliminates no one and elevates everyone. But no matter how unpopular this alternative notion of power, it is the only way for groups to transcend their selfishness, resolve their conflicts and manage their affairs in a way that does justice to everyone involved.

The essential problem in any situation of injustice is that one human being is exercising control over another and exploiting the relationship of dominance. The solution to the problem is not simply to reverse roles in the hope that once the roles have been reversed the manipulation will discontinue. The solution is for people to stop trying to control each other.

All of us, to one degree or another, exploit the opportunity if we have control over another person's life. Common sense therefore dictates that the solution to the problem of exploitation cannot be through the traditional notion of power with its emphasis on controlling others. The solution must lie in the alternative which emphasises controlling ourselves individually and collectively.

Some of us sincerely believe that if we are to help people, particularly the oppressed, we need to manage their affairs for them. But it doesn't matter how we try to rationalise it, controlling others always empowers us and disempowers those we seek to help. The only way people can be helped, particularly the oppressed, is for them to be empowered to take control over their own lives.

This is why Jesus explicitly forbade his followers taking control over others, no matter what the circumstances. Their job was not to seek control, but to enable others to take control over their own lives. (Matthew 20:25–28)

It is a pity that many of us who claim to follow Jesus have not followed his advice. We could have been saved the inquisition and the crusades. It is an irony that the greatest example we have in modern history of someone who did act on Christ's advice did not claim to be a Christian. We desperately need more people who will experiment with non-violent revolution as Gandhi did.

Let me tell you about one of my own feeble efforts to put this principle into operation.

As mentioned previously, we live in Brisbane's West End, the location for World Expo 88. Hundreds of low-income families were made homeless as landlords sold their rental properties for redevelopment or jacked up rents to cash in on the influx of visitors.

People in West End had fought the establishment of Expo in their suburb for five years . . . in vain. The State Government steamroller crushed public criticism. But the people had to deal with more than a powerful State Government. They had to deal with a whole array of power brokers who were scrambling for Expo-related profits. An unholy alliance of greedy landowners, real estate agents, development groups and government agencies moved in for the kill and people felt powerless to stop them.

Like everybody else, I also felt powerless. The irony is that as long as I thought I was powerless, I was so. However, through prayer, I began to realise I was not without power and I had a responsibility to do something to solve my part in the community problem.

The most popular idea for solving this community problem was to identify the tenants as the goodies and the landlords as the baddies, and to mobilise the tenant/ goodies to fight against the landlords/baddies in the hope that the tenants/goodies could force the landlords/ baddies to capitulate to their demands for cheap, secure accommodation.

Some even suggested a style of guerrilla warfare, led by chain saw wielding storm-troopers who would cut the power brokers down to size – a prospect so horrifying that the solution was worse than the problem.

A much less popular idea was to identify the destructive forces of greed at work in all of us and to encourage people of all classes to deal with those forces constructively by fighting collectively against our own greed and fighting for the needs of others. The problems with this idea were many. But at least the proposed solution, a quiet revolution, was not worse than the problem it purported to solve. So I opted for this less popular approach.

I decided to go on a hunger strike to fight against my own greed and fight for others' needs. I vowed to fast until fifty landlords agreed not to increase their rents by more than ten per cent, fifty tenants agreed to support responsible landlords and expose irresponsible landlords, and fifty residents agreed to help landlords and tenants negotiate just settlements, publicly commending those who did and publicly condemning those who didn't.

Two others joined me in my hunger strike. Every lunch-time we stood in the main street of West End, collecting the signatures of landlords, tenants and residents who agreed to work together to save our community from destruction.

Changes happened. One major landlord agreed not to raise his rents at all. Another landlord, responding to an appeal by his tenants over a raise in rent imposed by the real estate agent, fired the real estate agent and fixed the rents at the original rates. Yet another landlord, upon discovering that his tenants were going through a tough time financially, actually reduced the rents for a period of time. These landlords, and others like them, were presented with bunches of flowers in the main street of West End in order to commend publicly their sense of responsibility.

Two landlords, however, proved to be ruthless in their profiteering. We went and talked to them face to face about the consequences of their actions for others. They were completely unmoved. So groups of people camped on their doorsteps to bring home the reality of the homelessness they were creating and to condemn in public these landlords for their irresponsibility.

Both the presentation of flowers to responsible landlords and the camps on the doorsteps of irresponsible ones were featured on prime-time television.

Over the ten days of our fast, we collected more than 150 signatures of support from landlords, tenants and residents. So on the tenth day we broke our fast in public with a special meal at a local Lebanese restaurant to celebrate the solidarity, albeit partial and temporary, that had emerged again in the community.

The confrontation envisaged by the reactionaries would have exacerbated existing conflicts in the community. The tenants may have coerced the landlords into making concessions, but both sides would have been left with a hatred of each other and would have been increasingly hostile to each other. The real issue of greed in each of us would not have been dealt with at all.

Through the campaign we conducted, we sought to reconcile these existing conflicts in the community. The tenants and the landlords were converted to a common cause. Instead of fighting each other we attacked the real enemy . . . the greed in each of us.

From this experience we learnt the significance of the alternative notion of power Jesus advocated over against the traditional one to which most of us acquiesce. We learned that just two or three people, with very little support and very little help can be a catalyst for significant change.

It proves that we don't have to control others to bring

about change. Coercion is neither necessary nor desirable. Conversion, encouraged by affirmation of good and confrontation of evil, can be effective.

But it also proves we do have to be able to control ourselves if we are to bring about change in our society. We need to transcend our selfishness, resolve our conflicts and manage our affairs in such a way as to give everyone a fair go.

It's interesting to note that Jesus and his followers used organic images to describe the way the power of the Spirit, the power to manage our own affairs, operates in our lives. For example, self-management is described as the fruit of the Spirit. The power develops unobtrusively, as quietly as fruit growing on a tree. (Galatians 5:22)

That power may develop unobtrusively, but is far more significant than we may ordinarily imagine. Like a minute seed that seems so small that it could never amount to anything, the power of the Spirit always seems embarrassingly insignificant to begin with, yet always grows into something tremendously significant in the end. (Matthew 13:31–32) That power does not develop without opposition but like a plant growing in the midst of weeds, the power of the Spirit grows strong in an environment that could easily destroy it. (Matthew 13:24–30)

How the seeds of transformation that bear the fruit of the Spirit grow in a community is a mystery. (Mark 4:26–29) However, it is no secret that the seeds of transformation that bear the fruit of the Spirit will not grow in a community if those of us whose lives constitute those seeds do not bury ourselves in the life of our community. As Jesus said, 'Unless a seed falls into the ground and dies it produces nothing, but if it dies it will produce much to bring life to others.' (John 12:24)

All of this might sound like mystical nonsense, but it works in the nitty-gritty of real life. The disciples were a bunch of unorganised, uncouth, common people who couldn't have organised their way out of a wet paper bag.

Yet they turned their world upside down and started a movement that has been at the forefront of significant community change for 2000 years.

The interesting thing about this movement is that history shows that it is most often people like the disciples, the nobodies of this world, who bring significant change through the power imparted by the Spirit.

I once watched three young men, who like the disciples were considered nobodies, turn their community upside down. Larry, Emmanuel and Danny wanted to work with unemployed people in their neighbourhood. There were just three of them . . . and hundreds of dispirited unemployed living in extreme poverty.

The situation looked absolutely impossible. Larry, Emmanuel and Danny all had a history of mental and emotional disorders. They seemed very fragile, quite unreliable, and almost sure to be ineffectual. Those they sought to help had no marketable skills and many were chronically ill. They were not just poor; they were hopelessly destitute. Larry, Emmanuel and Danny had none of the qualifications that would normally be required for such a job. All the programmes that had been tried by the experts to help these people develop employment opportunities had failed. What hope was there for Larry, Emmanuel and Danny?

They had no cash; no skills; no helpers; no experience; no contacts in high places. Instead they decided to bury themselves and their ambitions in the life of the people of this neighbourhood. They did so in the hope (they didn't have a clue how – nor did anyone else) that by the power of the Spirit they could help these people help themselves with one of the most difficult tasks of community work – employment.

They prayed with the people for hope. They spent time together exploring options. They experimented with different programmes . . . and failed. But they refused to give up. One day someone came up with the idea of recycling garbage. It was the right idea at the right time. A garbage recycling co-operative was formed and the community got to work.

Anyone who has anything to do with co-operatives knows they can be fraught with incredible difficulties. This one was no exception. It was fraught with every difficulty imaginable – from nightly rivalry to daylight robbery. And in many ways the venture was an utter failure.

But for the first time in a long time, some of the people in these slums had a basic income that helped provide for the basic needs of the whole community. Through the co-operative, people in the community who had been debilitated through destitution, developed confidence in their ability to gain and maintain control over their lives in spite of the immense difficulties they still faced. These dispirited unemployed people began to experience profound personal growth and social change through the power of the Spirit.

What were the ingredients for such success in the midst of such failure? Rubbish . . . and three fragile young men, without a lot of money or large numbers of people to help, who simply sought to enable people to manage their own affairs effectively in the power of the Spirit.

What resources did Jesus use in his work in the community? He got together a few ordinary people who didn't have a lot going for them but who were empowered by the Spirit to manage their own affairs in a way that gave everyone a fair go.

IDEAS FOR MEDITATION, DISCUSSION AND ACTION

1. **Recall**: What resources will make the difference between success and failure in dealing with the issues in the community you want to address?

2. **Reflect**: How would Jesus encourage us to utilise these resources?

3. **Relate**: Why is the power of the Spirit so important for us in recognising and utilising our resources?

A HEART FOR BREAKING
THROUGH BARRIERS

7

BREAKING THROUGH THE BARRIERS OF FUTILITY

If you have ever tried to break a life-controlling habit, tried to help a friend with their addiction or tried to break through the entrenched greed that stands in the way of social justice, then you will have discovered that in the end your greatest enemy is an overwhelming sense of futility.

You will have discovered a closed system of programmed actions and reactions, cultural conditioning and bureaucratic red tape that are so interlocked they seem to present an impregnable fortress. Others before you have tried to break through. You have tried to break through. Nobody believes anyone can break through. It's business as usual.

I telephoned a pastor of a local church recently and asked him about the possibility of getting his congregation involved in community work in our neighbourhood. 'No chance!' he responded. 'Most of the church people don't even live in this area. Those who do are so busy with church activities they wouldn't have time anyway. Besides, they're not that type. They don't even open the door of their house to me, their pastor, let alone a stranger from outside the church.'

The pastor expressed the sense of futility we have all experienced when we've attempted to persuade people to change. The pastor expected me to bow before this futility and admit defeat just as he had.

Jesus faced this same sense of futility.

On one occasion, a rich young man came to Jesus asking

what he could do to help Jesus's cause. 'Sell all you have and give the money to the poor,' was Jesus's response. The rich young man just turned and walked away. Jesus then commented to the disciples about how hard it was for the rich to get involved in his movement of social transformation. 'It is easier to squeeze a camel through the eye of a needle,' he commented sarcastically.

At this point Jesus felt the futility of trying to convince the rich to redistribute their wealth to the poor. It seemed like an impossible dream – just as impossible as the pastor thought it would be to get his capable yet complacent congregation to change radically enough to get involved in their neighbourhood. But Jesus simply refused to accept the impossible as impossible. 'What is usually considered impossible,' he instructed the disciples, 'is possible to God.' (Luke 18:27)

As far as Jesus was concerned, the impossible was possible. It was possible for the rich voluntarily to share their resources with the poor so that no one in a community would be in need. But as far as the disciples were concerned this was just a utopian dream. And while they believed it was such a dream it remained one. What was needed was for them to begin acting on the possibility that the impossible was possible. When they eventually did, the utopian dream became a practical reality. The rich began sharing with the poor – voluntarily!

In the early church community in Jerusalem, the rich sold their excess land and possessions and shared the proceeds with the poor. Luke, in his record of those days, says, 'No one claimed that any of his possessions was his own, but they shared everything they had . . . There were no needy persons among them.' (Acts 2:43–47 & 4:32–37)

While it is true that utopian dreams can be transformed into reality, we must beware of naivety . . . a belief without doubt which ignores facts and lives in a world of foolish optimism.

I can remember the times I believed I could change the world – all by myself. I was optimistic. But my optimism blinded me to the essence of the struggle for change. We must grow beyond such naive optimism.

At the same time we must beware of cynicism . . . doubt without belief which rejects faith and lives in a world of futile pessimism. I can remember the times I doubted the world could ever be changed. Pessimism gripped me. I couldn't even change myself; let alone the world! Pessimism debilitated me, sapping the strength I needed for the struggle for change. We must not only grow past naive optimism. We must also grow past cynical pessimism.

One of the things that disturbs me most is that many of us have our naive optimism knocked out of us very quickly. This is replaced by cynical pessimism which takes much longer to overcome. Some of us never get out of it at all; we are left paralysed by an overwhelming sense of futility.

We must grow into a new maturity. A maturity which neither rejects faith in the possibility of change nor ignores the facts that say change is impossible, which acknowledges the difference between dreams and realities; yet recognises the difference God can make in turning utopian dreams for the community into a practical reality. We must begin to live as if the impossible is possible, because unless we do, nothing will change.

Some cynics may tell me I am naive in my believing that the impossible is possible. I don't think I am, because there are many times I have doubted I could change my world. But in spite of these doubts I believed I could live my life in such a way that would contribute to a changed world.

And the impossible has happened. My wife says I have changed – maybe not much, but at least a little. And my friends say the changes in me have helped me change my world – maybe only partially and temporarily but significantly nonetheless.

The cynics would say for me to believe this proves I am naive! Maybe I am. If so, so be it. But I would prefer to be a naive fool who at least tries to do what ought to be done than a cynical sage who does nothing but criticise those who try.

In spite of what the pastor told me about the impossibility of getting his congregation involved in community work in our area, I persisted. I didn't give up. I kept on going. Yes, doors were shut in my face. But other doors were opened. I talked to people about the possibility of being involved in our community. And people did respond. One here and another there. The people started doing what the pastor said was impossible.

The most worthwhile community work is done when we do what we are tempted to believe is impossible.

How do we break through the barriers of futility?
By growing beyond naive optimism and cynical pessimism into a maturity that acknowledges realities yet believes that with God dreams can come true.

IDEAS FOR MEDITATION, DISCUSSION AND ACTION

1. **Reflect**: What do we imagine may be God's dream for our community?
2. **Relate**: How could we make that dream come true?
3. **Respond**: What action will you take to make that dream come true?

8

BREAKING THROUGH THE BARRIERS OF SELFISHNESS

Our culture celebrates selfishness

How often have you heard this piece of folk-wisdom? – 'You've got to look after number one. If you don't, no one else will.'

In our society selfishness is sensible. We are a consumer society. Competition is the means, profit the end. Charity begins at home – but never extends any further. But then nobody really expects it to.

Nobody would seriously debate the degree to which selfishness has pervaded all sections of our society. One might hope that the church would be different, but sadly it displays the same preoccupation with self.

Recently I was talking to a young lady from a fast-growing, suburban church. She oozed confidence and enthusiasm for life. But what disturbed me was that this enthusiasm was all directed at herself. She was preoccupied with herself, her business and her success. Unfortunately, this young lady typifies the self-involved spirituality that is rampant in the church. A spirituality that prays for a parking space but drives past people stranded in the rain. A spirituality that spends millions of dollars building church edifices for spiritual self-gratification, but ignores the plight of the homeless.

I challenged this young lady about her selfishness. She disagreed, got angry and sped off in her BMW.

We must confront this selfishness which is celebrated by society and condoned by the church if we are to get beyond greed and meet needs. And the place to start confronting selfishness is in ourselves.

Jesus called for us to make serious decisions about our life style if we want to be part of a movement for justice. He insists we opt out of consumerism. 'Do not worry about what you can get to eat or drink.' (Matthew 6:25)

Jesus insisted we stop 'eating and drinking to excess' and start 'hungering and thirsting for justice'. (Matthew 5:6) Justice will not be done in our communities by having a TV dinner in front of a documentary on street kids. Justice will be done by turning the television off, getting out and meeting the kids on the street and inviting them home for a meal.

So how on earth do we deal with our selfishness?

Selfishness cannot be dealt with by engaging in more analysis of self. It is ironic that any effort to deal with selfishness by introspective reflection only makes us more selfish. We become preoccupied with our own improvement as a person . . . and that is essentially selfish.

Selfishness can only be dealt with by giving up our preoccupation with ourselves and giving ourselves wholeheartedly to the service of others. Jesus dealt with selfishness by allowing God to set the agenda for his life – an agenda of service to others.

Jesus showed how he allowed his Father to set the agenda for his life when he said, 'I don't do anything of myself, or for myself, or on my own account. I only do what I see the Father doing.' (John 5:19) 'I have food and drink that you don't know anything about. My food and my drink is to do the Father's will.' (John 4:32, 34) And Jesus showed clearly what the Father's agenda was for his life when he said, 'I have come not to be served, but to serve, and give my life to the people around me.' (Matthew 20:28)

I am convinced that for me to be involved in community work, I must deal with selfishness. But the selfishness I must start with is my own. For me that means making decisions every day of my life about my priorities. Decisions, not for myself, but for others. Decisions that are in sympathy with God's heartbeat for my neighbours.

One way I have found useful in dealing with my own selfishness is to start each day with a period of prayer. My first task during this time is consciously to tear up my own shopping list of what I want God to do for me. I rip it to shreds and throw it away. My second task is to take a blank piece of paper and start writing down the things I believe God wants me to do for him in the community.

Sometimes the ideas that come to mind are the obvious. But the issue is not whether the idea is obvious or not but rather whether it is something I ought to do or not.

This morning that meant getting up early to make tea for my wife and breakfast for my children. It meant helping get the kids off to school as well as getting ready for my own work that day. It meant contacting people I knew needed help. Occasionally the ideas that come to mind are not obvious.

One morning I awoke with the idea that I should visit a sick, lonely man who lived in our neighbourhood. I had tried many times to visit him before – but always in vain. I could never catch him at home. I had virtually given up hope of ever seeing this man. I knew he had been very ill and was desperately in need of friends who would care for him, but what more could I do? I had done my best.

So when I awoke with this nagging feeling that I should visit this neighbour, my natural instinct told me I would be wasting my time. But in spite of my doubts, I obeyed the Spirit's prompting and before work, strolled across the road to make an unscheduled visit. He was at home. The call was a tonic for him and for me.

The most worthwhile community work is done when we decide to put our own needs aside and simply do the good we know we ought to do for others.

How do we break through the barriers of selfishness?
By letting God set our agenda, giving up our preoccupation

with ourselves, and giving ourselves whole-heartedly to the service of others.

IDEAS FOR MEDITATION, DISCUSSION AND ACTION

1. **Reflect**: What agenda do we consider God might have in mind for us to do?
2. **Relate**: How can we get these things done?
3. **Respond**: Which of these things will we start with right now?

9

BREAKING THROUGH THE BARRIERS OF FEAR

Recently I spent a number of weeks talking to a church about becoming involved in their local community. Discussions had gone well. The congregation had identified a number of needs in their local community and explored methods of meeting them. But when it came to the acid test of putting the plans into operation, their enthusiasm suddenly evaporated.

'Why?' I asked them in astonishment. 'Because we are scared,' they replied.

'Have you met some of the people around here?' they explained. 'If we visit those people, chances are they will visit us. Then we'll never get rid of them. They'll just hang around the house.'

Fear of the unknown. Fear of failure. Fear of the cost to personal security and private space. Even fear for safety. Whatever the fear, it stands like a school-yard bully ready to challenge all those who dare cross the line to fight for the underdog.

Jesus was no stranger to fear. When large crowds surrounded him, he knew the threat they could be to him. He had no illusions about a fickle public. John says that Jesus didn't trust the crowds because he knew what was in their hearts (see John 2:24–25). He knew how they could use him. He knew that eventually they would turn against him and execute him.

But although there were times Jesus didn't trust people, there was never a time he didn't care for them. Jesus looked beyond the threat and saw their need. Instead of recoiling in fear, he reached out and embraced them. He enabled the very people who would betray him to live fuller lives.

Jesus overcame his fear by developing a compassion for people that was more powerful than his concern for himself or his own safety. When confronted by a man with gangrenous leprosy, Mark says, 'Moved with compassion, Jesus reached out his hand and touched the man.' (Mark 1:41) Jesus's compassion overcame his fear of catching the disease.

This compassion was inspired by listening to his Father's heartbeat. He knew how much his Father was pained by the suffering of his children and he was willing to risk his own life to relieve that pain. But his compassion was also inspired by his exposure to the needs of those he had chosen to live with. 'He became flesh and dwelt among us.' (John 1:14) Not only did he choose to live among the common people, he chose to live like a common man; subject to the same hardships and hassles. 'Though he was rich, yet he became poor.' (2 Corinthians 8:9) 'He was tempted in every respect as we are.' (Hebrews 4:15)

In the end Jesus overcame fear by being more afraid of what would happen if he didn't get involved than if he did. To watch the continued oppression of the poor from a safe distance and secure vantage point was a far more terrifying prospect than joining them in their struggle and sharing in their suffering. To compromise his ideals was more frightening than to be killed for his ideals. The death of his soul was more terrifying than the death of his body.

Fear of involvement in the community can be dealt with as Jesus dealt with it. Many of our fears are fears of the unknown. They are based on ignorance or prejudice rather than fact. These fears can be dispelled simply by coming to terms with the facts. Actual knowledge of our neighbours, no matter how different they may be from us, often dispels any fear of becoming involved with them.

A friend of mine was wanting to get involved with a person with a handicap. But he was afraid of becoming involved because he felt awkward around people with handicaps and didn't know how to relate to them. However after spending some time with his disabled neighbour, he discovered his disabled neighbour was just like him. The fear, based on ignorance, disappeared in the light of this knowledge.

Fears based in ignorance or prejudice can be dealt with as Jesus dealt with them. By living with people and getting to know them as people. But while some fears have no basis in fact . . . some do.

One night I was walking down the street and came across a man being attacked by a group of men with a broken bottle. His face was covered in blood. If someone didn't intervene it appeared he would be cut to shreds. I knew I should intervene but I was also tempted to walk on. I was afraid. And my fear had a strong basis in fact. There were two of them and only one of me. I had no weapon. They had a broken bottle.

Such fears cannot be dealt with by denying their reality or denying their cause. We must simply gather the courage that enables us to do what we know must be done in spite of our fears. So I gathered all my courage, crossed the road, and with much trepidation, intervened in the fight.

We can develop our courage by developing our love for people. If our fear is greater than our love for them, we should try to enhance our love in prayer until we are more afraid of letting them down than we are of their putting us down.

In the case of my intervention in the fight, I became more afraid of what the two men might do to their victim than what they might do to me. The danger to my soul if I did not act was greater than the danger to my body if I did.

The most worthwhile community work is done by people who act in spite of their fears.

How do we break through the barriers of fear?
By getting beyond ignorance and prejudice and caring
enough to have the courage to get involved in spite of our
fear.

IDEAS FOR MEDITATION, DISCUSSION
AND ACTION

1. **Reflect**: When we think of the things God wants us to do, what are we most scared about?
2. **Relate**: How can we overcome this fear?
3. **Respond**: Which of the things we have been fearful of doing will we do today?

10

BREAKING THROUGH THE BARRIERS
OF REACTION

Our civilisation functions on the principle of reciprocity
and retaliation – the pay back system.

'You scratch my back, I'll scratch yours.'
'An eye for an eye and a tooth for a tooth.'

We are told we are to treat others just like they treat us. If
they do us a good turn, then we should do them a good turn.
If they give us a hard time, then we have a right to get mad.
Mad enough to get even. Vengeance is right. Intimidation
is smart. Mercy is stupid. And a smack in the mouth for
someone who's crazy enough to call us names is nothing but
pure poetic justice.

Nothing stands in the way of creative involvement in the
community more than the cycles of reaction this pay back
system sets in motion.

One pastor said to me, 'Unless those people cross the
threshold of the sanctuary, I'm not prepared to waste my
time on them.' A priest once assured me, 'We don't mind
those people using our church facilities, but if they break
anything we'll kick them out quick smart.' Another pastor
told me, 'We are evaluating our community service programmes. Those that have not produced enough converts
compared to the effort we have put in will have to be
chopped.'

All these comments indicate a willingness for people in
the church to get involved in the community . . . on their
terms. And what are their terms? There must be a payback

and it must be positive. If there is no payback, or the payback is negative, then they may not return evil, but they will certainly withdraw from doing the good they could do. If that means some people are left to suffer, an effective evil for evil retribution, then that is tough luck. They should have played the game.

But the spirit of vengeance not only pervades society and the church. It affects you and me.

There is only one way to break its power. We must decide to follow Jesus's example and be proactive rather than reactive, returning good for evil rather than evil for evil. Only by breaking out of the payback system can we take the initiative for peace and justice.

If we are to be involved in our communities in a creative way then we must get beyond being reactionary, treating others as they treat us, and become revolutionary, treating others like we would want to be treated. As Jesus said, 'Do unto others as you would like them to do to you.' (Luke 6:31)

Jesus actually insisted that we 'Love our neighbour as we love ourselves . . .' in spite of how they may treat us. We are even to love our enemies. 'Love those who hate you. Bless those who curse you.' (Matthew 5:44)

Our communities can never be changed until the cycles of action and reaction are destroyed in our attitudes, habits and behaviour. There will be no change until we are committed to a revolutionary concern for others which does not depend on receiving good in return and is not diminished by having bad returned for good.

Jesus urged his followers to be like his Father 'who causes the sun to shine on the sinners and saints alike and sends the rain upon dishonest and honest alike.' (Matthew 5:45)

To do evil for good is demonic. To do evil for evil is human. To do good for evil is divine.

Therefore we must exorcise our demonic tendencies to vent our frustrations in a destructive way; transcend our human reactions to avenge any violation against us; and call on the divine to help us renounce all evil and use the energy released by our outrage when evil is done (either to us or those we care for) into constructive acts of love.

Jesus was well aware of the difficulty of following this path. It would mean giving ourselves to those who might be ungrateful for our help and rip us off into the bargain. It would mean being willing to suffer violence rather than inflict it. So he counselled his followers to 'give . . . and not expect anything back.' (Luke 6:35)

He suggested we develop an attitude of forgiveness, no matter how many times the same person may rip us off. 'If your brother does you wrong seven times a day, and seven times a day comes back to you and says he is sorry, forgive him.' (Luke 17:4)

He was even so bold as to suggest that 'if anyone hits you on the cheek, turn the other.' (Matthew 5:39) We must be so committed to the principle of good for evil that we are willing to die rather than kill. 'You must disregard yourself and be ready to die.' (Matthew 16:24)

Sure there are limits. But Jesus suggests it is not up to us to set them. We must give, forgive and suffer till we have exhausted every human reserve . . . then ask God for the strength to give, forgive and suffer some more. We are to give as long as it meets someone's need. We are to forgive as long as it sets someone free. We are to suffer as long as our suffering creates the chance for a human being to be born again.

We have reached the limits of our usefulness in doing good for evil only when our giving or forgiving makes us irritable, our suffering makes us resentful, or our generosity makes others incorrigible.

If we become irritable or resentful, Jesus said we must pray for grace to extend our capacity to give and forgive in spite of how much we may suffer. (Luke 6:32–36) However, if the people we are relating to are incorrigible in their mistreatment of us, Jesus said we should confront them face to face and work it out with them. (Matthew 18:17) Jesus says, if it works out we should continue to hang in there with them, but if it doesn't, we should forget about it and move on psychologically if not physically. (Matthew 10:23)

Jesus calls us to be willing to lay down our lives gladly to help people but he doesn't expect us to be locked into violent relationships that don't help anyone at all.

Ange and I are painfully aware of the need to be pro-active rather than reactive. We constantly monitor our responses to situations so we are aware of our reactions and can rectify them.

One morning I awoke to find Ange talking to herself in the mirror. She was just sitting there muttering to herself.

I thought she had cracked.

She had been under an enormous amount of pressure over the past few months trying to help a lady who was going through a tough time. Ange had worked with the lady night and day and was totally exhausted. The lady had made dramatic changes which everyone attributed to Ange. Everyone that is except the lady herself. She had abused Ange and told everyone in the neighbourhood that Ange had not done enough to help her.

So when I saw Ange talking to herself in the mirror I thought the pressure must have finally got to her. I rolled over a little closer to see if I could pick up what she was saying, and this is what I heard. 'No matter what she may do to me, no matter how hateful, she can't make me hate her. I will not hate her. I am going to love her no matter what she does. No matter how long it takes. God give me the strength.'

Ange stuck to her word . . . for a whole year. Finally her love broke through the hatred and a beautiful friendship flowered.

Pain is always involved in doing good for evil. We must be willing to accept the pain inflicted on us as the price we are prepared to pay to see our communities transformed.

Strangely enough it is often the people who need our help most who cause us the most pain. They desperately want our help but they must test our sincerity. We must accept the pain as part of the price of proving our sincerity. The size of the test usually depends on the size of their suspicions. And the size of their suspicions usually depends on how badly they have been ripped off in the past.

Ange and I decided that we should try and befriend some of the folk who live in the run-down boarding houses in our area. So one day we called into one of the boarding houses and met an alcoholic.

Now we had really gone out of our way to meet this man. The boarding houses were a couple of kilometres from our house. We had interrupted a busy schedule to visit. We went to his house. We offered him friendship. We offered him our time. And what did he do?

Abused us! For two hours he told us what he thought of people like us who don't care for people like him. People like us were quite happy to see people like him rot in their rooms alone. We didn't deserve one ounce of respect.

Like anyone else, we were tempted to storm off and never return. If we had obeyed our natural instincts, that would have been the end of the story. But we didn't. We went back to him again and again. Slowly his anger subsided.

One day I met him on the street and he stopped me to talk. The next day he came to visit us at our place. Shortly after he invited us to his place for a party, not as strangers, but as his special friends.

Unfortunately, those we are helping will not be the only ones who cause us pain. We must also learn to accept pain from those who sit on the sideline and abuse those willing to get involved.

The more we became involved in our neighbourhood, the more abuse we copped from certain quarters of the church for doing stupid things like going to a booze-up put on by our alcoholic mate instead of doing sensible things like giving out religious tracts to the drunks on skid row.

One day Ange and I got word about someone we considered a friend telling people behind our back about how far off the track we were with our involvement in the community. We analysed the criticism and decided not to react. We would not reply to the gossip. Instead we would wait for an appropriate opportunity to get our critic off the sideline and get him involved.

During the next six months the gossip increased. It was terrible. Not only were we getting a hard time from those we sought to help, but we were feeling put down by the people in the church who we thought would support us.

Then one day we got word that the person who had started the rumours had helped someone in our community. This was our opportunity. I phoned immediately. But not a word did I breathe about the gossip or how hurtful it had been. Instead I congratulated him for getting involved in his neighbour's plight and encouraged him to keep up the good work.

The effect was remarkable. Two days later we heard from mutual friends that the phone call had encouraged him to become more involved in the community. He even went so far as to suggest that the church should get behind what Ange and I were doing in the community.

The struggle for justice can be lonely. Friends don't always understand. But the pain of alienation is part of the price of proving the credibility of our ideas and the integrity of our commitment. The most worthwhile community work is done when we resolve to do good . . . in spite of any evil done to us.

How do we break through the barriers of reaction?
By being proactive rather than reactive; doing good regardless of the evil done to us; and accepting the pain involved as the price we're prepared to pay to do good for evil.

IDEAS FOR MEDITATION, DISCUSSION AND ACTION

1. **Reflect**: Who are the people God reminds us need our friendship but because of the hard time they have given us, we want to avoid?
2. **Relate**: How could we try to become their friends?
3. **Respond**: What will we do to become their friends this week?

A HEART FOR BUILDING BRIDGES

11

BUILDING BRIDGES TO PEOPLE

When we returned from India, one of the cultural differences that struck us most was Australia's preoccupation with privacy. In India the average family (by family I mean mum, dad, six kids, grandma, grandpa and maybe an uncle and aunt) live in a single room the size of most Aussies' garages. In India Ange and I shared our house with up to fifty people at any one time. From time to time we had to share our bedroom with other married couples. On occasions we even had to vacate our bed for people going through crises.

Back in Australia, we stayed with Ange's mum and dad for a year. Ange's parents are part of a large Greek community and enjoy a similar culture of sharing as we had experienced in India. But we soon discovered that what was true for the Greek community in Australia was not true for the rest of Australia.

The preservation of privacy has become a sacred duty for most Australians. The degree of social distance in Australia must be among the greatest in the world. Planting the Anglo-Saxon preoccupation with privacy in Australia's vast open spaces gave birth to a culture, not only in the outback, but also in the cities, which expects people to respect each other's space, keep their distance, and not invade other people's privacy. A culture that advocates the building of six-foot-high fences to protect neighbours from each other's friendship and preaches a superficial mateship which is held together with large quantities of amber liquid.

Recently I dared to suggest that in our society, the only

good neighbour is a dead one. Those listening were out-raged. But the fact is that when I ask people about their neighbours they often say, 'Oh I have wonderful neigh-bours. I never see them or hear a peep from them. They don't cause me an ounce of trouble.' Which either means they live next to a cemetery, or as far they are concerned, their neighbours are as good as dead.

When we moved into our present neighbourhood, we visited all the people in our immediate area. The range of reactions was amazing. Some welcomed us. But many peered through the curtains, not daring to open the door, or opened the door but remained safe behind the security grille.

One day I greeted one of these neighbours in the street. 'What are you?' he growled at my friendly g'day. 'A real estate agent or something?' The tragedy was that this man could only conceive of someone offering friendship . . . if they had something to sell. There was no place for a neighbour who just wanted to pass the time of day.

It is often people in the church who prove my neighbour's suspicions right. Religious people are notorious for not having time for their neighbours, except, of course, when the neighbour becomes the subject of a religious duty called evangelism – the selling of our brand of religion.

So how do we build bridges that span these deep chasms of alienation which divide our society and prevent any attempt at building a united, caring community?

To begin with, we need to develop an identity that makes us an integral part of our community. It is possible to live in a local community but not become a part of the identity of the local community. It is only as we are accepted as a 'local' that the bridges of friendship can be built over the chasms of alienation.

Jesus recognised the importance of this process. For thirty out of the thirty-three years of Jesus's life, he was just the bloke next door in a nondescript village called Nazareth. But it was there that he 'grew in favour with God and man' . . . building a credible local identity.

Even when he began his public life, he deliberately played down his superstar status. He wanted to remain a bloke next door so people would not be alienated by extravagant claims of his importance. (Mark 1:25, 43–44, 8:29–30)

Unfortunately many followers of Jesus concentrate on the last three years of Jesus' life and ignore the first thirty. During the last three years he addressed the needs of the community, but it was in the first thirty that he developed a common life with his neighbours that gave him the credibility to speak out on the issues that affected him as well as them.

We remember the three years in which he spoke out on community issues but forget the first thirty years when he was taught the culture, learned the language, developed relationships, picked up the stories circulating around town, and deeply heard those who were hurting.

Many of us feel that all there is to speaking out on issues that affect our communities is to speak out. But it isn't. Jesus earned credibility as a neighbour in a local neighbourhood before speaking out. Without this local credibility our statements will lack substance and significance.

There can be no substitute for the long process of building a credible, local identity. This is the foundation for any bridges we might want to build in the community.

This process starts with the way we introduce ourselves to others in the community. How we do this lays the foundation for the bridges we want to build. By emphasising what we have in common, rather than those things that separate us, we can lay a strong foundation on which to build.

This may seem obvious enough but many of us don't do it. We often emphasise those things that separate us rather than those things we have in common. Consequently we blow up the very bridges we are trying to build.

For example, a pastor from a local church recently complained to me that their church had visited everyone in the neighbourhood and had got zero response.

'How did you introduce yourself?' I asked him.

'As members of the local Baptist church,' he said matter of factly.

'Even to Orthodox and Catholics?' I asked.

'Of course,' he responded.

'To Hindu and Muslim?'

'Yes.'

'To atheists and agnostics?'

'Naturally.'

'My friend,' I said, 'you only have yourself to blame. You cannot introduce yourself to people as someone different and expect them to treat you the same as a friend.'

To identify with your neighbour, you must introduce yourself in terms of those things you have in common. I am a member of a Baptist church, but I never introduce myself to anyone as a Baptist unless they are also a Baptist. To the Orthodox and Catholic I identify myself as a follower of Jesus. To the Hindu and Muslim I identify myself as a believer in God. To the agnostic and atheist I identify myself as a student of Truth.

In my neighbourhood I am simply a neighbour. But establishing a credible, local identity involves far more than introducing myself as a neighbour. It means *being* a neighbour. And that takes a lot of time, time I never seem to have. I always seem to be too busy to be neighbourly. I have to make the time. For me it is a constant struggle to make sure I'm not too busy to be neighbourly.

There are two types of time we can use for building bridges in our community; scheduled time and casual time.

1. Scheduled times are planned meetings that are dominated by the **clock** and usually **formal**.
2. Casual times are opportune moments that are **event** orientated and **informal**.

Both kinds of contact are essential for building bridges in the community. Scheduled, formal contacts are a way of connecting us with representatives of groups we may not normally have access to and may give us access to the resources of the group they represent. Casual, informal contacts are a way we can turn our connections with people into friendships which enable us to relate to one another, not in terms of our respective roles, but as fellow human beings.

Unfortunately most formal meetings build walls of alienation rather than break them down. The formality of proceedings often holds people apart. People relate to each other, not on the basis of their common humanity, but on the basis of their formal roles.

If formal meetings are to break down the walls of alienation rather than build them, the formality of the proceedings needs to be interspersed with informality so people can relate to each other, not only on the basis of their formal roles, but also on the basis of their common humanity.

We may live in a modern society dominated by formal meetings rather than a traditional society dominated by informal gatherings, but all of us are still intuitively aware that it is in our informal encounters that the real business of relationship building takes place.

There are times in all of our lives when we are more open than closed to contact with others. Unfortunately, most community groups (including the church) are so dominated by their schedules that they are not flexible enough to respond to these opportunities that arise with the ebb and flow of life.

These opportunities for developing caring relationships often pass as quickly as they come. They must be grasped immediately or lost forever. We must be flexible enough to respond to these opportunities as they arise. It is at these moments we must make the conscious choice to schedule in time . . . or throw our schedule out.

Times of change, cycles, crisis, celebration or chance encounter are the times when even the most closed in our society open themselves to the possibility of meaningful friendship. These are our opportunities to build bridges with people in the community.

Change.　Starting a new job or moving house are times of change when old relationships are disrupted and new relationships established – a time when people are more open than usual to making contact with others. The openness created by this change usually lasts from a few days to a couple of months. But once a person becomes familiar with their surroundings, they tend to close off again.

Cycles.　The cycles of life also bring with them the opportunity for new or renewed relationships. For example, everyone loves to show off a new baby. You can stop a total stranger in the street and chat with them about their toddler. Everyone loves to talk about their kids.

When the kids first start school it is easy to make contact with the other parents dropping off their children. And when they finally leave school, it is easy to talk to other parents about their concerns for the future of their kids.

Engagements and weddings are public events that provide opportunities to open relationships that have been closed or even to establish a friendship with someone we don't know very well.

If someone with whom we have a strained relationship is suffering the loss of someone they loved, it is an ideal time to rebuild the bridge of friendship through sympathy and practical support.

Crisis.　There is nothing like a fight at the factory or a feud in the office to bring people together. Ironically, fights can often break down the walls of alienation. Having to resolve a conflict can build bridges between people who never had to relate to each other before. For instance, in our neighbourhood we recently had a dog pooh dispute that had everyone hopping mad. Large dogs were leaving large deposits in everyone's front yard and the owners seemed loath to take any responsibility. The dispute acted as a catalyst to draw our neighbourhood closer together as we struggled to find a mutually acceptable solution.

Celebration.   At parties people are just as happy to talk to a total stranger as talk to old friends. The multicultural fiestas held in our neighbourhood each year are a fantastic opportunity to appreciate each other's traditions and culture. Religious festivals such as Easter and Christmas are ideal times to meet other people and experience their traditions and spirituality. Secular festivals, like national holidays, provide opportunity to explore our commonality as fellow citizens.

Chance encounters.   Often people feel safer in a chance encounter. They don't feel set up. After all, the very nature of the meeting is unpremeditated. For example, some time back I met a neighbour at the supermarket checkout. I'd seen him around before, but always felt awkward about approaching him because he seemed very nervous about meeting people. But here at the checkout we met quite naturally. He was obviously at ease. So I chatted with him about the price of groceries – and so began a friendship.

But often these opportune moments come at inopportune times. Recently we were getting ready to go out when we heard a commotion in a neighbour's back yard. Looking out the window we saw two neighbours, who had been at loggerheads for years, embroiled in a fight. This was a time of crisis, an opportune time to get involved further with two of my neighbours. But my day was already mapped out. What should I do?

Throwing my schedule away, I jumped the fence and picked up Lesley whom Jimmy had just knocked to the ground. I then told Lesley and Jimmy that they really needed to settle their differences before they ended up doing serious injury to each other. So I invited them to come up to my place, have a cup of tea and try and sort it out sensibly.

I spent several hours helping them resolve their differences. I then prayed for each of them and when I finished they were both crying. Both of them gave me a big hug and said I was their best mate. All of which could have been missed had I been unwilling to dispense with my schedule and seize the opportune moment.

If we are to build bridges in the community, we must build when the time is right. And the time is right when other people are receptive to the bridge being built. The time is always dictated by the others, never by us. The time to build is not when we are ready, but when they are ready. We can build most bridges when we are most sensitive in recognising opportune moments and most ready to scrap plans in order to grasp those opportunities.

Jesus placed his emphasis on informal involvement with people. Even the little formal involvement he had was always at the mercy of the informal. His schedule was always being rearranged so he could grasp the opportunity presented by the unexpected. Jesus's frame of mind is best summed up in the story that he told about the good Samaritan.

A traveller lay beaten on the side of the road. There was never a better time for the priest and the pastor who passed by to build a bridge of friendship than at this moment of need. But both were too busy with their religious duties to respond. A Samaritan who passed by was not too busy to care and grasped the opportunity with both hands.

It is clear from this story that Jesus understood that such caring could be costly. Grasping the opportunity was a costly business for the Samaritan. His schedule was severely disrupted by stopping to help. He exposed himself to possible danger from the bandits, who, for all he knew, may have still been lurking nearby. And he had to pay a hefty hospital bill for the now destitute traveller.

But Jesus indicated to his audience that this is the price all of us should be willing to pay in order to build bridges to people in need in our community.

How can we build bridges to people that overcome the alienation in our community?
By laying a foundation of a credible, local identity and then

building on that foundation by using every opportunity to develop formal and informal contacts with people.

IDEAS FOR MEDITATION, DISCUSSION AND ACTION

1. **Reflect**: What do we have in common with the people in our community?
2. **Relate**: What opportunities are there to develop our relationships with them?
3. **Respond**: What time will you set aside to get together with your neighbours?

12

BUILDING BRIDGES ON RELATIONSHIPS

By and large our society operates on superficial relation-ships. We ostensibly build bridges of friendship to each other, but want little or no involvement with each other. Instead we play games with each other. The purpose of these games is to appear that we are involved in the lives of others without actually getting involved.

We all know the rules; keep the conversation shallow but pretend it is deep and meaningful; talk about yourself but tune out when others talk about themselves; use the in jargon but make sure there is no genuine meeting of the souls.

Religious people have their own variations on these games. As a friend of mine, a migrant, who has stopped going to his local church says, 'Religious people love to play a game called "church". We dress up, go through a ritual, and whoever looks the most pious wins. The prize is approval. Then we all go home and wait for next week's game. No one gives a damn about being really involved with each other.'

The people at this church go home convinced they have had meaningful contact with each other and have provided real help for my migrant friend. After all, they did pass the peace and had a cup of tea and a chat after the service. But my friend feels that even though he made the effort to meet people on their territory and on their terms, the encounter was totally superficial. The banal chatter bore no relevance to the loneliness of the boarding house room to which he was condemned for the remainder of the week.

The tragedy is that even if most Christians were to visit my friend on his territory, the lonely boarding house room, we would still not be able to relate to him on his terms. Instead most of us would play a piety game or a proselytisation game.

The object of a piety game is to convince ourselves and others of our virtue. The piety game is characterised by judging ourselves and others on the basis of petty issues. It is not concerned about meeting people at their point of need, but using their needs to make them look bad and us look good by comparison. The piety game prevents a genuine encounter in which we can come to terms with our common needs together.

The object of a proselytisation game is to convince as many people as possible to join our cause. In the proselytisation game we treat people as faceless commodities – potential trophies for us to win. We do not treat people as people. If we meet people's needs, it is not so much to help them, but to help us win them over. The proselytisation game may promote encounters with people but subverts the possibility of developing relationships of mutual acceptance and respect.

Many of us, realising the destructiveness of the piety and proselytisation games, give up playing religious games. But few of us give up playing games altogether. For instance many of us get into fad games like the welfare game.

The object of the welfare game is to appear as if you are involved with the needs of the community without actually getting too involved. If you play the game well, you can get a lot of credit without paying the price of costly involvement. The game begins when a group is challenged about being involved in their community. The group can't say no because they would be denying the voice of their conscience. But on the other hand they find it hard to say yes because of the cost.

To resolve the dilemma, a committee is appointed to do the job for them. And the committee appoints a professional to do the job for them. The game is played with a number of variations but the aim is always the same – to get the credit for being involved in the needs of others without actually getting involved.

For example, a church may be challenged to provide support for elderly people in the community. Instead of the church members personally providing the support their elderly neighbours need to stay in their own homes, the church appoints a committee which erects an old people's home, and hires professionals to care for the senior citizens on their behalf. The church can fly their flag over the project, the committee can get accolades at the annual general meeting, and the professional can get the feeling of a job well done. But at no stage is anyone expected to take their elderly neighbours into their hearts or their home.

The problem of the welfare game is a problem of all games – they alienate us from one another because not only do some win and some lose; those who win, win at the expense of those who lose.

Jesus refused to play games. He scathingly criticised people who played piety games (Matthew 23:23) and proselytisation games (Matthew 23:15). And roundly condemned those who pretended to be on about the welfare of others when their only concern was for their own. (Matthew 23:25).

Jesus developed a non-game playing way of relating to others in which no one would win at the expense of anyone else. The non-game playing relationships he promoted meant nobody won unless everybody won, and if someone happened to lose, then everyone shared in their loss. The non-game playing relationships brought together the very people that the game playing relationships had kept apart.

Jesus developed an authentic heart to heart connection with people. The bridges he built with people carried two-way traffic – an uninhibited exchange of pain, anguish, disappointment, joy and expectancy.

The story of the woman of Samaria is the classic example of how Jesus built bridges with people and encouraged them to share their needs.

When the woman of Samaria arrived at the well, she was intent solely on discussing such mundane duties as drawing water from the well. Jesus kept trying to make it a more meaningful discussion. The woman tried to keep the conversation shallow by pretending to make it deeper than it was. She tried the theological ploy. She tried to embroil him in a theological discussion on the difference in worship styles between the Jews and Samaritans. But Jesus refused to play the game. He side-stepped the debate on their theological differences and moved the conversation forward to a genuine meeting of their souls. She told him her heartbreak. And he took her heartbreak to heart.

Like Jesus we need to build bridges that give people the opportunity to meet us halfway, share their hearts and meet each others needs.

I remember the day I met Prem, an Indian who had come to Australia to study. He was a stranger in a foreign land, estranged from his country, his culture, and his religion. When I met him and he discovered I could speak his language, he was thrilled. But when he, a Sikh, found out I was a Christian, he was afraid I might try to convert him. It would have been very easy for us both to play the piety or the proselytisation game and never develop a genuine friendship. However, I embraced him, not as a potential trophy, but as a fellow seeker after truth. I explained that we were both in a pagan environment and that we needed to support each other spiritually to survive. I suggested to him that to do this he should tell me stories about Guru Nanak and I would tell him stories about Guru Jesus. From this common ground we built a bridge of friendship across the chasm of religious differences that enabled us to meet halfway, share our hearts and meet each other's needs.

We can start to understand what kind of bridges need to be built by studying the reported needs in our community. Federal, state and local government, welfare organisations and voluntary groups, universities, colleges and libraries all carry records and research that will help us understand our communities better. National departments of surveys and statistics provide valuable information on population, health, education, economics, employment, religion and ethnicity of all local areas.

We can learn valuable lessons about how to build these bridges by discussing the reported needs with leaders in our community who are reputedly trying to meet these needs. Politicians, police, medical practitioners, ministers of religion, consultants, teachers, social workers and community workers can help us understand some of the complexities of trying to meet the needs in our community.

But we will never actually build bridges, a heart to heart connection with those in need, till we meet with people face to face. This means getting together with people to talk about ourselves, our families, our past hurts, our hopes for the future, the needs we perceive, and the way we could meet these needs together.

The young people at our local church recently built some bridges with the older people in our community. They decided to act when they discovered from the census data just how many older people there were in our community. The census data also indicated that many of these older people lived on their own in rented accommodation. The young people approached the older people in the church to talk about the problems they faced. They then went with 'Meals on Wheels' to visit the older people in the community who never came to church to discuss their needs face to face.

The youngsters were horrified by the conditions that many of these people lived in. Many lived in damp, dingy dwellings. Most never went out. Few, if any, ever got visitors. All had jobs they couldn't do themselves that desperately needed doing.

The young people became determined to do what they could to help these older people. They sent out notices through 'Meals on Wheels' and put up notices in doctors' surgeries offering their help. The notices said, 'There will be no charge for labour but a cup of tea would be appreciated.'

The young folk have cleaned up yards, gone shopping, scrubbed floors, washed dishes . . . and had numerous chats with the older people over numerous cups of tea. In talking to both the older people and the young people, it's hard to tell what they value most. The job well done . . . or the cups of tea.

How can we build bridges on relationships that overcome the superficiality of the games we usually play?
By developing an authentic heart to heart connection with others which enables us to meet halfway, share our hearts and meet each other's needs.

IDEAS FOR MEDITATION, DISCUSSION AND ACTION

1. **Reflect**: With how many of the people from our community that we get together with do we have a heart to heart connection?
2. **Relate**: How could we meet more of them half-way, share our hearts, and meet one another's needs?
3. **Respond**: What initiatives will you take to get beyond the superficial to deepen your relationships with people in the community?

13

BUILDING BRIDGES THROUGH GROUPS

In modern society, independence is considered a virtue and dependence is considered a vice.

Even when we talk to each other, an attitude of isolation still exists. We may even talk about our problems – but we want to solve them *alone*. Even if we seek help from others, we are merely asking for advice on how *we* can solve *our* problems by ourselves.

Our culture celebrates the individual to the detriment of the collective. We avoid dependence like the plague. Dependence of any kind is weakness, whether that be other people being dependent on us, or us on others.

Even though our insistence on independence appears liberating, it is in fact debilitating. Like a branch broken from a trunk, we become cut off from the love, wisdom and strength that flows in the corporate tree. The break is never clean. Not only do we lose the sense of being a part of a community, but we also lose the part of ourselves which can only be fully alive while we are part of a vibrant community.

Is it any wonder therefore that we cannot solve many of our problems? Cutting ourselves off from one another is not only the cause of many of our problems but also cuts us off from creative solutions that can only be found in strong community life.

In my experience, we in the church are often more blinded by individualism than people in the wider community. Not only have we been shaped by the same cultural values as the rest of society, many of us have adopted a theology which reinforces our individualism rather than diminishing it.

This stress on the individual is strongest in the pietistic churches where over-emphasis on personal salvation, personal conversion and personal sanctification rationalises a preoccupation with the individual at the expense of the collective.

Jesus grew up in a close-knit Jewish village. Group life, where people could draw on love, strength and wisdom in order to resolve their problems, was of enormous importance to him. He did most of his work with people in groups.

Jesus started with existing groups: ranging from conservative groups like the local Hebrew synagogue in Nazareth to radical groups like that led by his cousin John in Jordan.

But Jesus also set up his own groups on the edge of existing groups; close enough to enable ongoing relationships with existing groups but far enough away to allow for experimentation not normally allowed in the existing groups. Jesus also sent out people to start other support groups, with local people and for local people. (Luke 9:56)

Most of the great work Jesus did was through small groups. Individualism was not replaced by collectivism or independence by dependence. Instead, a healthy *inter*dependence was encouraged which nurtured people's potential, enabling them to blossom as people in the life of an integrated community.

Ange and I have learnt the importance of doing community work through groups. We start with existing groups. Some groups are informal, like our family and friends. Other groups are formal, like the government department that looks after youth and family welfare. Some groups are conservative, like the church we attend. Other groups are radical, like the community of anarchists we associate with in our area.

All of these existing groups have strengths – areas in which they meet needs efficiently. We work with these groups in those areas because it would be folly to set up a group to meet needs that these groups are already meeting.

But these groups also have weaknesses – areas in which they fail to meet needs effectively. By definition the most needy people in our neighbourhood are those whose needs are not being met by existing groups. For their needs to be met, either established groups must be altered or alternative groups must be established. Often this means setting up other groups to model the change required.

These emergent groups may be just inside or just outside existing groups. They must be close enough to enable ongoing relationships, but far enough away to allow experimentation.

Ange and I try to set up such groups on the creative edge of existing groups. For example, I recently encouraged a congregation I was working with to disband their women's fellowship to start a support group for single mothers under stress. Recently Ange developed a support group to provide self-help for women who have been victims of abuse and brutality. This group was established on the edge of a large congregation which already provided crisis accommodation.

Starting a support group can be both surprisingly easy . . . and infuriatingly difficult.

Jesus suggested it could be as easy as two or three people recognising a common concern. He suggested we begin to work out our common concerns for the neighbourhood over meals in one another's homes. (Luke 10:7)

At times this search for people with a common concern can be extremely difficult and frustrating. Search as we may, we just can't seem to find someone whose heart beats in harmony with ours. These are the times for quiet determination to keep looking. Times for heeding the advice of Jesus, '. . . keep looking and you will find.' (Matthew 7:7)

We need to look among people we already know who may be interested. We should talk to these people about our concerns, sharing our heart with them. They may think we are crazy. But on the other hand, they may share our concerns.

We should also explore existing groups that may be engaging in activities closely related to those we are interested in. When three people decide to work together on a community concern, then a group has formed.

Starting a group can be difficult, but never as difficult as the task of **maintaining** the group.

Power struggles are the most common cause of the destruction of groups. Jesus suggested the way to deal with this was for there to be no bosses in a group but for everyone in the group to be a worker who works for the welfare of the group. (Matthew 23:8)

Of course all groups need leadership. But Jesus's idea of being a leader had nothing to do with control. For him, being a leader meant being a facilitator. He said that in support groups, 'the leader should be the servant'. (Matthew 23:11) Not controlling the group. But facilitating.

Understanding the development phases that all groups pass through can be helpful to facilitators. The most commonly recognised phases are forming, storming, reforming and performing. **Forming** is when the group first gathers around a common concern. **Storming** is when the group tries to find solutions to the problems. This usually involves a sequence of stormy disputes. **Reforming** is when these disputes are resolved and the group finds a practical way forward. **Performing** is the carrying through of agreed strategy. All groups pass through these phases and in any dynamic, growing group, these phases will occur over and over again. Facilitators are aware of these phases. They initiate when the group is forming. They conciliate when the group is storming. They consolidate when the group is reforming. And they co-ordinate when the group is performing.

Groups must be developed with a lot of care if they are going genuinely to help people grow. They must be open not closed, inclusive not exclusive, co-operative not competitive, small not big and all the members of the group must be active not passive.

Because of the time and energy that groups require, it is important that we limit the number of groups we are involved in. Those of us operating in the local community in the context of a local church probably need to restrict ourselves to operating through just three groups – one larger group for meeting together and two smaller groups for nurture and mission.

We are involved in our neighbourhood through a local congregation. Once a week we meet as a large group of people who share a common faith and common life. During the week we are involved in a cell group that meets to nurture our involvement in the local community in the light of Jesus's example. Once a week we also meet with a community group which gives us the opportunity to be involved in a mission together – the developing of networks of friendship with migrants and refugees in our neighbourhood who are otherwise friendless in a foreign land.

For the original inhabitants of Australia, much of this type of group work was as natural as the tribal environment in which they grew. For our society, which has largely despised tribal values and destroyed tribal culture, it is an incredible irony that many of our modern Australian dilemmas can only be solved if we develop traditional, Aboriginal methods of group process.

How can we build bridges through groups to overcome the isolation in our community?
By developing interdependence through support groups, starting with existing groups and establishing alternative groups where existing groups are not meeting community needs.

IDEAS FOR MEDITATION, DISCUSSION AND ACTION

1. **Reflect:** Who do we know who might be interested in meeting the community needs we are aware of?
2. **Relate:** How could we support one another in this?
3. **Respond:** What action will you take to participate in such a group, if a support group already exists, or develop such a group, if a support group needs to be established?

14

BUILDING BRIDGES FOR CO-OPERATION

It is one thing to get people to co-operate with one another in a group; quite another to get the group to co-operate with other groups. Misunderstanding, suspicion and competition make sure that most groups keep a safe distance from each other and move only in their own circles.

One might hope that the church, which preaches reconciliation, may be an exception. But experience shows the opposite is often the case. In fact ecclesiastical groups are often even more irreconcilable than secular organisations.

Last year a Christmas celebration was sponsored by an alliance of local churches. It was a combined, interdenominational, cross-cultural, multi-lingual celebration of the coming of Jesus held in the street, right in the middle of our suburb. The hundreds who attended were enriched by a moving service, rich in the contrasting colours and textures of the various religious traditions represented.

A week later, an evangelical church which had boycotted the combined event, put on an event of their own. But without the combined support of the other groups they were unable to secure a suitable venue or secure sufficient support. The event boycotted by the evangelicals was phenomenal. By contrast the event staged by the evangelicals on their own was pathetic. Virtually no one was there – except the few they had brought along.

The evangelical church rationalised their decision not to co-operate with the other churches. Having been raised as an evangelical, I know the arguments inside out. Most of the arguments are based on misplaced notions of purity reinforced by prejudice. These are the very same arguments that the Pharisees used to justify their separatist stance in society – a stance vigorously attacked by Jesus.

Jesus encouraged everyone to co-operate with everyone regardless of the group they belonged to. He deliberately encouraged the orthodox to support activities promoted by those they considered heretical, as long as those activities were characterised by love and justice.

Once a religious academic asked Jesus for an authoritative definition of a 'neighbour'. In response, Jesus told the story we mentioned earlier known as 'The Good Samaritan'. A man, battered by robbers and left to die by the roadside, was ignored by representatives of the religious establishment but was helped by a Samaritan, a man regarded by the religious establishment as a heathen. Jesus then instructed the religious academic to get beyond being religious and start doing some good, like the Samaritan. The idea of a good Samaritan was repulsive to the religious academic. For the Jew, the only good Samaritan was a dead one. Jesus's instruction for the Jew to work with the Samaritan in doing good was equivalent to his telling Christians to join the Communists in doing good in the community. A horrifying thought for most Christians. But then Jesus would never have made a good Christian, would he?

Jesus made no apologies for stressing the importance of working together as neighbours – even with those we consider to be enemies.

When Jesus sent his disciples out to do community work, he suggested they find others they could work with. There were just two qualities Jesus said his disciples should look for in the people they wanted to work with. They needed to be peaceful and hospitable. In other words, co-operative. He said nothing about the disciples checking out their religious views. (Luke 9:5–6)

When the religious leaders of Jesus's day criticised him for associating with people whose religious beliefs were dubious, Jesus simply replied that he had come, not to call the religious, but to call the irreligious to the challenge of doing God's work in the community. (Matthew 9:13)

But even Jesus's own disciples had their problems in relating to other groups. One day they stopped a man doing good in his local community – because he didn't belong to their group. Jesus was appalled at their narrow-mindedness and reprimanded them for their short-sightedness. 'Don't stop him,' Jesus instructed them, 'because (whether they belong to your group or not) whoever is not against you, is for you.' (Luke 9:50) 'If someone is doing the same as us, they won't be quick to criticise us.' (Mark 9:39)

For Jesus, the possibility of co-operating with those with differing viewpoints was not a prospect to withdraw from, but an opportunity to be grasped with both hands and fully embraced.

Ange and I try to follow Jesus's example by drawing together groups who are willing to work together for the welfare of the community. We try to develop co-operation between various cliques in our congregation and between the various congregations in our neighbourhood by calling people together to consider common concerns.

Recently Ange's family invited a wide range of people to come to their house. As people entered, they put a pin in a large photographic map on the wall to indicate where they lived. They then shared with the group the concerns they had for their neighbourhood and what they were trying to do about them. People then broke into small, mixed groups to discuss their efforts and pray with each other.

That such a meeting happened in our area was a minor miracle. Those invited came from a range of groups who were traditionally hostile to each other. There were Protestants and Catholics, Charismatics and Conservatives, Evangelicals and Orthodox.

Out of that meeting grew a sense of togetherness in our struggles for the local community that made future co-operation much more feasible. As a result, every Friday morning, people from the local Anglican, Catholic,

Uniting Church, Greek Orthodox, Greek Evangelical, and even a couple of Baptists, meet together prayerfully to explore ways of implementing God's agenda for love and justice in our neighbourhood.

As George Lovell has demonstrated, it is possible to develop co-operation between various groups whether that be in the church or in the local community. Churches can begin by allowing **their premises to be used by other groups**. For example, the Catholic church in our area allows its premises to be used as a school for Aboriginal children and as a centre for Indo-Chinese refugees.

The advantage for those of us in the church is that we are forced to consider our relationship with the groups we share our facilities with; in the example above, Aboriginal children and Indo-Chinese refugees. The advantages for others is obvious; they get to use a facility which is usually over-protected, under-utilised and much needed.

The disadvantage is not the danger of damage that such groups may inflict on our property – a danger which Jesus indicated we should gladly bear. (Luke 6:32–36). The greatest disadvantage is that because we have allowed these groups to use our premises, we somehow feel we have discharged our duties to the community. The temptation is to feel we are more involved in our community than we really are.

It is possible to allow our premises to be used by other groups, yet have virtually no contact with the group at all – except when it comes time to collect the rent or pay for damages. Allowing our premises to be used by others may be the place to start our co-operation with other groups, but it must never be the place we stop. Churches can:

1. **Help administer a programme with an already established community association which needs support.** For instance, the local Anglican church allows its premises to be used by an already established community organisation, 'Meals on Wheels'. Besides offering its premises, a number

of people in the congregation are involved in the day to day running of the organisation.

2. **Help initiate or participate in establishing a local community association to provide a needed service.** For instance, the local Uniting Church has set up Family Care Services which provide assistance for families needing support by providing a community centre where people can just drop in. The centre also provides play groups, informational resources, educational courses, training programmes, counselling and referral services and community development. The Uniting Church initiated Family Care Services and has continued to participate by not only providing the premises but also by being involved in the committee that co-ordinates the service.

3. **Help personalise otherwise impersonal organisations.** For instance, many people who are entitled to claim social security are afraid to do so because they find the red tape and forms daunting. One church I was involved in accompanied such people to the Department of Social Security. The fact that only four out of a congregation of forty had jobs meant that the church had lots of people with lots of experience to provide this service!

4. **Help negotiate between aggrieved people and the organisation responsible.** People in the church I am involved in have made effective representations to the real estate agents on behalf of tenants who have been in danger of being unceremoniously turfed out of their apartments by callous and unscrupulous landlords.

5. **Help individuals involved in the community either by providing a support group in the church or sponsoring a support group in the locality.** A church in our area provides a support group for a lady who works with families whose children are abused. Another church in our area sponsors a support group for parents who want to develop their parenting skills.

How can we build bridges of co-operation that overcome the misunderstanding, suspicion and competition between groups in our community?

By determining to co-operate with any other group working for the good of the community and building bridges of co-operation between these groups.

IDEAS FOR MEDITATION, DISCUSSION AND ACTION

1. **Reflect:** What other groups besides our own might be interested in meeting the community needs we are aware of?
2. **Relate**: How could we co-operate with one another in this?
3. **Respond**: What action will you take to develop co-operation between groups in your neighbourhood so as to meet community needs better?

A HEART FOR BRINGING
GROWTH AND CHANGE

15

BRINGING ABOUT HOPE

How do you impart hope to the woman contemplating suicide because the man she loves is having an affair with a younger woman?

How do you impart hope to a man who as a child was abused by his father and now finds himself doing the same to his own children? He loathes himself, he loathes his actions, but he is gripped by apparently uncontrollable urges that erupt without notice.

How do you impart hope to grieving parents whose only son has been killed by a runaway truck?

How do you impart hope to a whole community of people whose homes are to be demolished to make way for a freeway?

If we are going to facilitate authentic transformation in our community, then we are sure to be confronted by the hopelessness that grips those who struggle to cope with the debilitating realities of their life.

I teach courses in community work. Most of the students seem hopeful. But when we begin to talk about the possibilities of authentic individual or collective transformation, the discussions inevitably bog down in total despair. And those who seem to know the most about themselves and their society are often the most despairing of all.

Without hope there is no motivation even to attempt change. It is therefore absolutely crucial that before any personal growth or social change occurs, people must experience hope in the midst of their hopelessness.

But how? Prayer was a process Jesus used to introduce hope into hopeless situations.

One day Jesus got an urgent message from two close friends, Mary and Martha. Their brother Lazarus was dying. By the time Jesus made the long journey to their village, the situation was hopeless. Lazarus was dead. In fact, Jesus had even missed the funeral and Lazarus had already been laid to rest in a tomb.

Jesus was overcome with grief. He openly wept and grieved with Mary and Martha. Going to the graveyard with them, he began to pray out loud. He deliberately prayed aloud so he could give voice to Mary and Martha's inner anguish, and in so doing, remind them that God was grieving with them.

As he prayed, the family gradually became aware that no matter how hopeless the situation was, there was still hope. Hope because, even in the midst of the tragedy of death, the source of life still existed and had the ability to bring life out of death. Which is what happened when Lazarus rose from the dead and strode towards the waiting arms of Martha and Mary.

Two very important principles can be found in this story.

First, Jesus entered into his friends' hopelessness. He did not laugh at their tears or analyse their grief. Instead he wept with them, fully embracing their grief. He did not try to promote hope until *after* he had fully partaken of their hopelessness. It is my conviction that prayers for hope are only meaningful to the degree that we have entered into the person's experience of hopelessness. It is only then that we can give voice faithfully to their cry to God and remind them that God will give heed to their cry. .

Second, the hope that Jesus promoted through prayer was not a fantasy experience that deluded Mary and Martha into believing they were better off than they really were. Instead, it was a faith experience in which the painful facts of their situation were miraculously transformed – bringing them face to face again with Lazarus whom they believed had been lost forever. I am convinced that prayers for hope are only liberating to the extent that they are prayers of faith rather than prayers of fantasy. Fantasy is a fixation on a particular outcome of the future which may or may not happen. But faith is a confidence in the possibility that either our situation can change, or that we can change enough to cope with the situation as it is.

This does not mean that faith is unimaginative. Quite the contrary. Prayers of faith involve encouraging people to imagine: either their painful reality being totally transformed; or alternatively, the pain remaining, and their being transformed through the pain.

Faith looks into the face of reality. Fantasy ignores it.

Jesus would have entered the realm of fantasy if he had encouraged Mary and Martha to imagine Lazarus rising and never having to die again. Instead, he imparted faith that imagined life coming out of death but accepted death as part of the process.

Therefore prayers of hope are only liberating to the extent that they face the facts yet allow for their transformation by God.

Like most people, I have not seen too many dead people get out of their graves. But I have encountered some of the greatest come-backs since Lazarus. I have often witnessed hope live again in communities where hope had died.

Recently a lady talked to me about the hopelessness that many people she knew felt as they struggled for authentic transformation. I wondered if Natalie was reflecting her own sense of hopelessness, but did not raise the issue. A few days later Natalie called on the phone. She was desperate. I dropped everything, went and picked her up and brought her home. When she arrived, we didn't need to talk about hopelessness. It erupted in our kitchen.

Ange and I embraced Natalie as she wept over the years of accumulated brutality that she had suffered at the hands of a drunken husband. We wept together, then prayed, voicing her pain to God. There at the kitchen table she breathed out the hurt and breathed in the healing.

That night we didn't get much sleep. Every time Natalie drifted off to sleep she would begin dreaming of the beatings and wake up screaming. She would leap out of bed and pace the floor seeking peace. By morning we were all exhausted.

For years Natalie had borne this pain alone believing that no one would understand. Even if they could understand, they could never share the pain. And even if they could share the pain, how could they ever help her rise from the depths of despair? But now she had spoken of her pain. We had provided the time and space for the pain deep inside her to surface in our presence. We had tried to understand and share her pain even if that understanding and sharing was imperfect.

Through prayer, Natalie began to face her pain without so much despair, believing that perhaps there was life beyond the death of all her hopes. And in the courage and strength that hope always imparts, Natalie has begun the difficult task of putting the pieces of her life back together again.

Not all sessions of prayer with people are as dramatic as the one with Natalie. People who are cynical about God may find such sessions strange. With such people, I ask them if I can pray and then pray as sensitively as I can. Sometimes I ask them to pray with me, using their imagination to sensitise themselves to possibilities they may never have considered.

In my experience, most people, even those who call themselves atheists, are open to my praying for them if I voice their cry faithfully, without patronising them, but with empathy and respect. Although these people often feel awkward to begin with, many actually feel that their cry has been heard and find new hope in the midst of hopelessness.

When praying with people, I pray with confidence, not that my wishes or the wishes of the person will be fulfilled, but that the facts of their situation will be miraculously transformed by God – bringing the person face to face again with a life they thought was lost forever when someone, or something, died.

It is not only important to experience the person's pain and hopelessness as you pray, it is also important to experience an infusion of hope on behalf of the person. More often than not, the person you are praying for will experience the same infusion of hope. It is then, and only then, that you can struggle with the person in helping them to put the pieces back together again.

How can we help people get beyond the hopelessness that debilitates them?
By entering into their hopelessness and, through prayer breathing life into the hope which has died.

IDEAS FOR MEDITATION, DISCUSSION
AND ACTION

1. **Reflect**: What kind of hopelessness do we encounter through our involvement in the community?
2. **Relate**: How can we help bring about hope?
3. **Respond**: What issues are you confronting at the moment that you can pray through with the people involved?

16

BRINGING ABOUT EMPOWERMENT

Hope alone cannot bring change. Hand in hand with hope must come empowerment. Hope is a fragile quality that is quickly destroyed by feelings of powerlessness. Hope inspires the possibility of change – but powerlessness induces despair. Unless feelings of powerlessness are dealt with, the hope infused today will be gone tomorrow.

Most of us are paralysed to some extent by a sense of powerlessness. Ironically, it is those who have tried hardest to bring change to the community who feel the most powerless. They know full well how the system is stacked against those who fight for change. If we are going to promote personal growth or social change, it is crucial to deal with this sense of powerlessness. We must enable people to realise their potential power in the midst of their powerlessness.

Jesus understood the causes of disempowerment. Self-doubt that debilitates us. Social indifference that under-utilises our inherent abilities. Traditional obligations that bind us. Political subjection aided and abetted by our own compromise and complicity with the *status quo*.

However, Jesus did not just discern the causes of disempowerment, he also indicated the sources of empowerment that would dispel despair and inspire people with the hope that they could make their dreams come true.

As discussed earlier in the book, Jesus saw power, not as the ability to control others, but the ability to control one's self. This meant controlling both actions and reactions. Empowerment then was the process of enabling people to exercise control over their own actions and reactions.

Sometimes empowerment happens dramatically, in an instant. Other times it happens almost imperceptibly, gradually over a long time. An example of the dramatic was the empowering of a man with a withered hand whom Jesus saw one Sabbath in the Synagogue.

To this man, his withered hand represented total powerlessness. Not only was it a frustrating physical handicap, it was a social handicap. According to the religious rituals of his time, his withered arm barred him from participating fully in the temple rites of his own religion. And because it was his right hand that was crippled, he would have to use his left hand for business as well as ablutions. According to the cultural traditions of the time, this meant he could never participate freely in the life of the town in which he lived. For him the withered hand was a handicap that not only debilitated him physically, but also spiritually, culturally, economically, and politically.

When Jesus saw this man at the back of the Synagogue, he called him forward and simply encouraged him to do what he had always wanted to do, but had been powerless to do – stretch out his hand. According to Luke, the man obeyed and his hand was restored.

In telling this story, Luke uses an interesting turn of phrase which emphasises that the restoration of the man's arm did not take place **before** but **after** he stretched out his hand. It was in the process of doing what the man knew he couldn't do that he was empowered. (Luke 6:6–10)

I have witnessed similar, dramatic instances of people being empowered. I remember once being at a party and some of our friends bringing a stranger with them. This stranger was so paranoid about meeting new people, he stood at the door too scared to enter. He was totally paralysed by his paranoia.

Another friend, Jack, realised the dilemma this young man was in so he left the party to talk to the stranger. Jack inspired in the stranger the confidence in his ability to do what he believed he couldn't – join the party.

Most instances of empowerment are not instantaneous. But whether instantaneous or long and tedious, the essence of empowerment is the renunciation of lies and the practice of truth.

Jesus insisted that it is lies that bind us and truth which liberates us. It is the lies we believe about ourselves that disempower us and stop us from changing. Conversely, it is the truth about ourselves that explodes our sense of powerlessness and sets us free to change. As Jesus said, 'You will know the truth and the truth will set you free.' (John 8:32)

Encouraging people to renounce the lies and embrace truth about themselves can be difficult and frustrating. It certainly was for Jesus. But Jesus persisted in the process of empowering disempowered people regardless of how long it took, or how arduous the process.

To those debilitated by self-doubt, who looked at Jesus as an example of what they would like to be but thought they never could be, he said, 'Anything I can do, you can do better.' (John 14:12)

To those debilitated by social indifference, who believed they could never make any difference because nothing ever changes, he said, 'Stop cursing the darkness. You are the light of the world. Those who do justice will shine like the sun.' (Matthew 5:14 & 13:43)

And to those debilitated by their obligations to tradition or their subjection to the *status quo*, who believed Jesus was right but that it was wrong to buck the system, he said, 'Forget about the system. Let the dead bury their dead. Followers of mine must be prepared to face the firing squad. Anyone who tries to preserve their life will waste it. But anyone who wastes their life for me and my movement will preserve the spirit that makes life worth living.' (Matthew 8:22, 10:34–39)

If we seek to be involved in empowering disempowered people, like Jesus we will have to encourage people constantly to renounce the lies that paralyse them or promote irresponsible, self-destructive action. In so doing we will have to encourage them to embrace the truth that will enable them to develop, and to act in a responsible, self-disciplined manner that allows them to take control over their own lives.

Ange, along with her friends, Renee, Carol, Donna and Jeannette, recently got involved with a group of people who felt totally powerless in our society. Some have had brain tumours. Others have had brain damage through strokes. Some are developmentally handicapped, while others suffer from psychiatric disabilities. All have been institutionalised due to their trauma and all feel that they cannot function adequately in the community without some kind of institutionalised support.

After meeting them, Ange and her friends were not only aware of the powerlessness of these people, they were also overwhelmed by their own sense of powerlessness. They were tempted to believe only professionals could help these people. How on earth could they help?

But the more they got to know these people, the more determined they became to find ways to help them. They renounced the lie that only professionals can help and embraced the truth that dedicated friends can help too.

The greatest struggle however was finding ways to empower these people who were thoroughly institutionalised. They made a number of decisions that proved crucial in this empowering process.

They decided not to come across in an overpowering way that would further disempower the people. They were determined to relate to each of the people as individuals, not as members of an institution, so that their personal identity was strengthened.

They committed themselves to help the people explore their own views, their dreams and their nightmares, in order not only to affirm their individuality but also to raise their consciousness about themselves.

They were concerned eagerly to confirm the truth and

gently confront the lies that emerged in their conversations with these people. They encouraged the people to renounce any delusions they had about themselves. And they encouraged them to embrace their own reality and take responsibility for that reality. And they sought to help these people develop their capacity for personal growth and social change through helping them realise the significance of the insights, values, knowledge and skills that they *already* had.

Ange and her friends believed that everyone involved could be empowered to become more fully human and alive if they worked together rather than working alone.

It would be lovely to say that as a consequence of their involvement that none of these people feel powerless anymore and all their disabilities have disappeared. But unfortunately this is not true.

Many of the people feel just as powerless as they did before Ange and her friends befriended them. But because Ange and her friends have treated them with respect, the people have become more respectful of themselves. Because Ange and her friends related to them as individuals, many of these people have begun to feel very special. In the context of this acceptance, these people have explored aspects of themselves that they had not come to terms with before. Particularly those parts of themselves which they felt guilty about and especially those parts of themselves which had caused others to reject them.

Some have made significant strides forward. Some have started to find greater solace in themselves than they found in the bottom of a whisky bottle. Some have started to develop independent living skills in preparation for moving into independent living situations in the community. Others have established interdependent relationships with people in the community characterised by mutual regard and mutual enjoyment. Others are beginning to realise something of their incredible potential to make a vital contribution to the life of the community through worship, service, work and play.

As they have renounced the lies that had left them powerless, these people have been able to embrace the truth of the power they hold in their own hands. Not the power to control others. But the power to control themselves and their own lives. That realisation has exploded their sense of powerlessness.

How can we help people get beyond the powerlessness that debilitates them?
By encouraging them to renounce the lies that disempower them and embrace the truth that empowers them to do the very thing they believed was impossible.

IDEAS FOR MEDITATION, DISCUSSION AND ACTION

1. **Reflect:** What kind of powerlessness do we encounter through our involvement in the community?
2. **Relate:** How can we help bring about empowerment?
3. **Respond:** What particular problems that appear impossible to solve can you enable people to deal with?

17

SOLVING PROBLEMS TOGETHER

Hope and empowerment are not enough to facilitate authentic transformation of our community. Even after hope has been infused and people feel empowered to take control of their own lives there is the nitty-gritty business of getting down to resolving problems.

A mechanical problem with a car can be solved once and for all. But problems in human relationships are never solved once and for all. They must be resolved over and over again by the people involved.

A community that is authentically transformed is not one that no longer has problems. Instead, a transformed community is one which has developed a process for resolving their problems in a fair way.

In fact, a community is transformed only to the degree that everybody in the community participates in creative resolution of their problems together. The very substance of authentic transformation is creative, community problem solving.

This raises an interesting question. As those trying to facilitate authentic transformation, what is our role in the problem-solving process?

It is instructive to look at the role Jesus played in settling disputes. Even though Jesus was unafraid to state his opinion publicly, when it came to stating his views on how a particular dispute should be settled, he often refused.

Whenever people asked him a question about a situation that projected the responsibility of answering the question away from themselves and on to Jesus, he usually refused to answer the question. He wanted people to own their own situation, accept the responsibility for their own problems, and accept the responsibility of resolving their own problems.

One day two brothers came to Jesus to settle a dispute over property. Jesus, in typical style, answered the question with a question: 'Man, who made me a judge . . . over you?' (Luke 12:14) Jesus used this question technique to make people answerable to themselves. It was often in the answering of a question that the person would be forced to take responsibility for solving their own problem.

While Jesus refused to allow people to project the responsibility for solving their problems on to him, he also stated quite clearly that they shouldn't project the responsibility on to anyone else either . . . particularly the experts. He actually warned people to 'beware of the experts'. (Luke 20:46) He told people *they* were the experts on their own problems. Instinctively they knew the answers. 'Why don't you judge for yourself what is right?' (Luke 12:57)

Jesus knew that nobody, no matter how expert they might be, could solve someone else's problems for them. Ultimately everyone has to solve their own problems. That is why Jesus insisted that if you have a problem with someone, you must deal with it 'between you and him alone'. (Matthew 18:15)

However Jesus also recognised that many of us need someone to help us in our struggle to solve our problems. The difference is that this person must act as a helper, not an expert. They are there to help us solve the problem, not to solve it for us.

Jesus said about problem solving, 'If a brother wrongs you, go and show him his fault, between you and him alone . . . But if he will not listen to you, take one or two others with you . . .' (Matthew 18:16). The role of these one or two others was not to take sides or give advice. They were there to help clarify the situation by enabling the various parties involved to listen to each other and talk about possible solutions.

Jesus called these third party helpers 'witnesses'. Their job was to bring the truth to light by faithfully declaring the facts as they saw them emerge from the murky shadows of the dispute. It was in this role of witness, rather than judge, that Jesus preferred to operate.

One day Jesus was teaching when a whole crowd of noisy people arrived dragging a woman who had been caught red-handed having an affair. They wanted Jesus to pass judgment on her. According to Jewish law, if this woman were guilty she had to be executed by stoning.

Jesus had gone on public record as being totally opposed to affairs. As a matter of fact Jesus had gone even further than the law of the land and claimed that if anyone even lusted after a woman he was guilty of adultery. It seemed an open and shut case. The woman had been caught in the act. The law required death.

But Jesus steadfastly refused to assume the role of judge. Instead he assumed the role of witness. When asked for his verdict he simply said, 'Let him who is without sin cast the first stone at her.' He witnessed to the truth, not only leaving her sin exposed, but also exposing the sin of her accusers. He then stooped and wrote on the ground with his finger, leaving them alone to make their own judgment. (John 8:7–8)

In allowing these men to make their own decision Jesus ran a grave risk. A woman's life was at stake. But Jesus, in spite of the risk, did not take the problem from them and resolve it for them. Jesus simply stayed with them and ensured they arrived at a loving solution which was fair and just to all involved.

The men made their judgment and one by one left. The woman was left alone with Jesus. Then and only then did he make his judgment. 'Where are they? Has no one stayed to condemn you?' he asked. 'No one, sir,' she said. Jesus responded, 'Neither do I condemn you. Go and don't do it again.' (John 8:9–11)

Jesus was prepared to make a judgment – but only in a

way that developed people's ability to judge for themselves.

If we are going to get involved in helping individuals or groups solve their problems, it will be extremely helpful if we understand the four phases in the problem solving process:

1. Define the problem.
2. Identify all possible solutions.
3. Choose an option and implement it.
4. Reflect on the results.

1. DEFINE THE PROBLEM.

The first question that must be asked before we can even start to look for solutions is, 'What is the real problem we are facing?' This is often the most difficult stage in problem solving. People confuse the symptoms with the cause. Often the problem is overlaid with unresolved past conflicts. As a witness, we must help those with the problem to get beyond a superficial view to a deep understanding of what the problem is. If we cannot agree on what the problem is, then we have no chance of agreeing on a possible solution.

2. IDENTIFY ALL POSSIBLE SOLUTIONS.

The second question we need to ask ourselves is, 'What are all the possible solutions to this problem we are facing?' At this stage it is a good idea to have a brainstorm of possible solutions. Each person thinks of as many possible solutions as possible and these are listed – no matter how whacky or crazy they seem. It is a good idea to ban all criticism of ideas at this stage so that people do not feel inhibited in bringing forward their thoughts and suggestions.

After the list is completed, it is time to look over each

solution more critically. This can be done by trying the idea out in our imagination. What would the possible results be if it were implemented? What are its weaknesses? What are its strengths? Is there some way it can be modified? There should be lots of discussion about each of the possible solutions. Disagreement will be healthy at this stage.

3. CHOOSE AN OPTION AND IMPLEMENT IT.

The third question we need to ask ourselves is, 'Which solution will we opt for and implement?' Those implicated in the problem must now agree on what they consider to be the best solution. The solution must be acceptable to everyone and everyone must be convinced it has a fair chance of solving the problem.

Once the solution has been chosen, the implementation has to be discussed. This involves discussing what has to be done, who will do what and most importantly when it will be done. It is a good idea to write down all the tasks that need to be done, and beside each task the name of the person responsible and the deadline they have agreed to. Options agreed to in principle are not agreed to at all unless these specifics are agreed to.

4. REFLECT ON THE RESULTS.

The fourth question we need to ask ourselves is, 'How is our plan to solve our problem working out?' Reflection must take place both during and after the implementation of the solution. During the implementation, people need to get together regularly and report on how they are going with their allocated tasks. Those involved need to discuss whether the programme is actually solving the problem or whether there needs to be some modification to the programme.

Sometimes the whole programme will need to be scrapped and the whole process started again. Before starting again it will be important to discuss what was learnt from the previous effort. Why did it fail? Were we treating the symptoms or the cause? Did it fail because the solution was wrong or because we failed to implement it properly? Experience shows that often people must be willing to try, try, try again before they eventually succeed.

When the solution has been fully implemented it is important to discuss the results. Each person should have the opportunity to say whether they feel the problem has been adequately solved. Each person should share what they have learned from the experience. Our role as witness in this problem-solving process is to help those involved work through the cycle sensibly and to be sensitive to the needs of everyone involved. Our job is to make sure no one loses and that no one wins unless everyone wins.

Recently Ange and I had a phone call from a young couple whose marriage was in a no-win situation. The husband had betrayed his wife by having an affair. Even though the husband deeply regretted the hurt he had inflicted on both the other woman and his wife, the damage seemed irreparable.

There were no winners, only losers. The husband had lost his integrity. The other woman lost her dignity. The wife lost self-respect and personal security. Together the husband and wife were about to lose their marriage. If the stress continued there was a good chance one of them may lose their mind as well.

So we invited them over. We sat and shared their grief and rage. Over the following weeks we spent days with them, weeping and worrying our way through the situation together. The last thing they needed was for us to take sides or give advice.

Ange and I knew we couldn't take the problem from them – as much as we should have loved to. They alone could solve it. All we could do was stand beside them and, in prayer, search for a way to resolve their problem so that even if they couldn't win anything, they wouldn't lose any more than they had already lost. It was a long struggle.

There were no quick fixes . . . just long days and longer nights.

It took time to define exactly what the problem was. There was a whole complexity of problems. Some his. Some hers. Some theirs. It took time to sort out the tangled web. They struggled to get beyond the symptoms to the causes. They found it difficult to agree on the causes of the problems that had combined to make their married life such a misery. It took time for their hurts to heal enough for them to be able to deal with their negative feelings about each other in a positive way.

In the end, the wife took courage in her hands, forgave her husband and gave him another chance. He took the chance, and together they began to rebuild their marriage. In fact they claim their marriage has become even stronger than before.

This example is appropriate, because marriage problems constitute such a large proportion of the problems needing resolution in our communities. There are not just marriage problems, but problems in families; not only in families, but also in institutions; not only in institutions, but also in society. And it is only in the resolution of such problems that authentic transformation in our communities can occur.

How can we help people solve their problems together?
By not solving the problem for them, but by staying with them, being a witness to the truth, and helping them work through the problem-solving process.

IDEAS FOR MEDITATION, DISCUSSION AND ACTION

1. **Reflect**: What serious community problem do we know of that needs to be resolved?
2. **Relate**: How can we help to bring about a resolution of this problem?
3. **Respond**: What are you going to do to encourage people to make some progress in resolving this problem?

18

PROPHETIC TRANSFORMATION

We have already noted that imparting hope is not enough to bring authentic transformation to a community. People need to be empowered to take control of their own lives. But empowerment alone is not sufficient if people still don't understand how to use that power to resolve their problems.

But even helping people solve their own problems is not enough. They may resolve the problem in such a way that it does not contribute to the long-term development of themselves or their community. In fact, the problem may be resolved in a way that yields short-term gains but long-term losses.

If authentic transformation is to occur, it is absolutely essential that people discover how to resolve their problems together in a way that yields long-term gains for everyone, even if it means short-term losses for the present.

In order for people to settle disputes, creatively and constructively, we need to enable people to solve problems together in the light of the prophetic tradition.

Throughout history there have always been prophets, both secular and religious, who have felt the heartbeat of God. These prophets courageously speak to us, in sympathy with God, about God's passion for love and justice. They call on society to make changes and solve its problems in the light of what God wants for this world and in the light of his concern for the underdog.

But history is the story of the silencing of the voice of the prophet and hence the silencing of the voice of God himself. Instead, civilisations have generally opted for short-term, selfish gains. But in rejecting the voice of God, history has become a tale of paradise lost, revolutions betrayed and lives wasted.

If genuine, sustainable transformation is to occur, we must enable people to solve their problems together in a way which takes into account the essential, visionary insights of the prophetic tradition. It is impossible to create a more loving and just society unless we take into account the agenda of love and justice advocated by sages throughout the ages.

Here is an example. Living at the time of Jesus were two men who had a problem they wanted to resolve. Both were super rich while most of those around them lived in poverty, struggling for survival. One was an aristocrat. The other an extortionist. Both felt uncomfortable about the disparity between their luxurious life style and the poverty they saw around them. Both decided they didn't like this discomfort and decided to do something about it. Both decided they would get a third party to help them solve their problem. Both sought out Jesus, a recognised prophet.

The rich young aristocrat ignored the advice advocated by Jesus. It may have been a good ideal to give everything to the poor but it wasn't a good idea for him to do so. Not that he didn't want to give to the poor. He just needed to keep a solid capital base to do it. He did not want to waste his capital on unprofitable charities. He probably rationalised his decision by arguing it was the most sensible course of action. He decided to solve his problem, not by giving away his wealth, but by simply refusing to feel guilty about it. If he had any guilt feelings left, I'm sure his priest and psychotherapist helped him cope.

The old extortionist on the other hand decided to handle his problem a different way. He followed the advice of the prophet Jesus. He gave half his wealth to the poor and repaid all those he had ripped off, not just what he had taken illegally, but four times what he had taken.

Both had effectively resolved their problem. One in response to the demands made by the prophetic tradition. The other ignoring it. In ignoring the advice of Jesus, the aristocrat chose a solution that denied the rights of the poor around him – the right to life. In choosing to disregard their rights, the aristocrat chose a solution that continued the cycles of poverty and oppression in his community. The solution gave him short-term gains, but long-term losses to his community.

On the other hand the extortionist, who had felt uncomfortable with his wealth, chose a solution which was even more uncomfortable – the giving away of his wealth. He did so, knowing that his short-term loss would be a long-term sympathy with God's concerns for the needy.

I am convinced that genuine, sustainable transformation can only be facilitated by enabling people to solve their problems together in the light of the prophetic tradition – perfectly personified in Jesus of Nazareth.

How can we facilitate this authentic transformation among people who are followers of Jesus?

When we meet together we encourage each other to share our problems and to help each other resolve these problems in the light of the prophetic tradition. We acknowledge the problems we are trying to solve. Then we discuss the issues with the people who share the problems we are trying to solve. Then we search the Scriptures in general and the life of Jesus in particular to discover a story that reveals how God may want us to resolve the problem in the light of his passion for love and justice. This process results in an intimate acquaintance with the heart of God which enables us to resolve our problems in a way that reflects the prophetic agenda of God.

But how can we facilitate such a process with people who are not followers of Jesus?

Let me tell you how I try to do it. Most of the people I work with for change in the community do not claim to be

Christians. In fact some are decidedly anti-Christian. But I agree to work with them on the understanding that our decisions be on the basis of common sense and consensus.

Because God is the source of truth, and that truth is written on the hearts of all people (Romans 2:14–15) and living in the hearts of all people (John 1:9), that truth is often expressed in the common sense we speak to each other.

Quite often, to the embarrassment of those Christians who claim exclusive rights to truth, those who do not claim to be Christian have a clearer understanding of the truth. Therefore, whenever somebody says something which I believe is true to the heart of God, I agree with it. If I do not believe it is in tune with God's heart, I disagree with it.

Just because I disagree doesn't automatically mean I will voice my disagreement. Conflict, like kisses, should be saved for special occasions.

The way I see it, every time I agree, I gain a credit in credibility. Every time I disagree I lose a credit. I want to gain credibility to discuss crucial issues – not lose credibility over incidental issues. I save my credits for the time I need to spend them on a disagreement that is substantive.

However, I don't find myself in disagreement as much as others might imagine. I find I can usually, if not invariably, agree with the way sensible people decide to solve their problems. The times I do find myself in disagreement, I feel perfectly free to express my thoughts because we have agreed to resolve our problems by consensus which means no one coerces anyone else into agreeing on any course of action with which they disagree.

Actually I find that many groups I work with, even those who only use God's name for blasphemy, often act in sympathy with his heart. That may seem strange to some. But it may not seem so strange if we remember that all of us, even those of us who don't believe in God, are made in the image of God, an image which though distorted, has not been totally destroyed by our proclivity to stupidity. So together we can agree to solve problems according to God's agenda – though at the time I may be the only one who recognises it as such.

Once we have resolved a problem and we are rejoicing together, I make explicit the implicit connection between the decision we have made and the prophetic tradition personified in Jesus. I love to tell people, particularly those hostile to Christianity, who are celebrating the successful resolution of a problem, that the success was dependent on our having taken the kind of action Jesus Christ advocated. Regardless of their attitudes to Christ, they cannot deny the successful resolution of the problem or disregard the value of the kind of action advocated by Jesus – especially when they have just tried it and seen how well it works!

I go through this process over and over again. Each time the group makes significant progress towards personal growth and social change, and each time I explain the significance of God's agenda personified in Jesus to the process we have just experienced.

As a result, God's agenda increasingly becomes a more credible point of view. Sooner or later, usually later, God's agenda, personified in Jesus, becomes such a credible point of view that it moves from being one point of view among many that are credible to the one point of view by which all others are judged. The indicator that this time has arrived is when people ask about God's agenda before they make a decision rather than after.

At this stage it is crucial to know enough about the gospels and the prophetic tradition to be able to find a parable, a story or a principle that relates directly to the problem the group is seeking to resolve.

If people adopt the agenda of God, personified in Jesus, as the agenda for their decision-making, they have made a significant transition. The agenda of God has moved from being a point of view to the point of reference. The process of conversion to Jesus as a person – not necessarily Christianity as a religion – has begun. And as part and parcel of this conversion process is the incredible potential for authentic, sustainable, community transformation.

Here is a story of how such a process took place among a group of people who were not only non-Christians but decidedly anti-Christian.

Together with my friends, we decided to get involved with a bunch of squatters. They were totally demoralised. They had no jobs. With no jobs they could not afford to pay rent. Because they had nowhere to live they squatted on land beside the road. Because this was illegal, they were constantly harassed by the police who would either demand a bribe, or break down their shanties and beat them up. As a result they were constantly on the move, trying desperately to stay one step ahead of the police. But there weren't many places they could go, so they always wound up back where they started, ready to go through the cycle again.

We got to know this group. Bonds of friendship formed between individuals and their families. They were demoralised, but what they lacked in dignity, they more than made up for in courage. Their struggle against seemingly overwhelming odds was fought with courage and lots of laughter. We were encouraged and strengthened by their style of heroism and infectious sense of humour. They may have been demoralised, but they taught us valuable lessons about the morality of survival.

As our friendships deepened, we not only learned from them the art of survival in an urban slum, we began to feel the anguish they felt in their struggle to survive. As we discussed with them the issues they had to face every day of their lives, we decided to work together with them and see if together we could find some long-term solutions that would not only minimise the anguish associated with their struggle for survival, but also increase their chances of surviving.

One day the group decided something had to be done about the continuing police harassment.

Some wanted to attack the police station immediately with bricks. Bricks were a common means of settling disputes in the slum. As a conflict resolution technique, the people considered it a knockout.

We encouraged the people to envisage in their minds what the result of throwing bricks through the window of the police station might be. They concluded that it would probably result in an even more violent visit by the police. The people began to have very serious doubts about the effectiveness of bricks as a conflict resolution technique.

So we began to discuss other possibilities for solving the problem. Someone suggested inviting the police over for a cup of tea and discussing the matter. The squatters treated the idea with scorn, but we supported it. The longer we discussed it, the more support it got.

Eventually the police were invited. To start with you could cut the air with a knife, but the tension was soon dispelled with a couple of jokes. The squatters and the police ended up having an amicable chat and as a result decided to call a truce. The squatters agreed not to cause the police any trouble and the police agreed not to beat up the squatters.

After the police had gone, we had a talk about how the problem had been resolved. During the discussion one of us mentioned that the problem had been resolved exactly how Jesus of Nazareth had suggested such problems be resolved. He said to 'bless those who curse you' – which is exactly what the group had done by inviting the police for a cup of tea.

Everyone treated it as a joke. They were embarrassed that they had done anything remotely religious, even if unintentionally. But the squatters remembered the way they had solved the problem with the police and they also remembered that it was the way Jesus suggested problems be solved.

Time went by. Week after week, month after month, we worked on a whole range of problems together. Everything from getting a regular water supply to improving nutrition and sanitation.

Each time we resolved a problem together it would be on the basis of common sense and consensus. After the effective resolution of each of these problems, we would discuss how the decision we had taken fitted with the way Jesus instructed that problems be dealt with.

After each successful resolution of a problem there would be a celebration. It was during this euphoria that we would always explain how the success was contingent upon our having worked in harmony with God's agenda, as reflected in Jesus. And always there would be mock groans and complaints that they would soon all be Christians before they knew it!

About a year after inviting the police for a cup of tea, the council decided to clean up the city. Cleaning up the city meant getting rid of the squatters. They were notified to leave immediately. But they had nowhere to go. Then they got news that really freaked them out. The bulldozers were on the way.

In a panic they considered their options. But there didn't seem to be any. Any promising options had to be discarded because they felt too powerless to make them happen. 'It's typical,' they concluded. 'Those big nobs can push us little blokes around as much as they like and there is not a thing we can do about it.' We were tempted to agree. Things looked hopeless. But somehow we knew that we had to believe that the impossible was possible.

'Surely there is *something* we can do,' a friend of mine said in a hopeful tone.

'Yeah?' said one of the squatters in a sneering tone. 'What? What would your mate Jesus do about it? What are you going to do about it?'

My friend who had made the suggestion sensed that this was a crucial time for this group. A time when Jesus might become more than just one point of view among many points of view. The time when Jesus might become the point of reference for all their problem solving. The time when the group might be converted to a faith in Jesus through which their life might be transformed. It all hinged upon finding in Jesus a story that the group could use to help them to do something about their situation. I also racked my brain wondering where on earth you could find a story in the gospels that helped a group of squatters deal with the threat of eviction backed by the might of bulldozers.

I don't remember who it was, but someone suggested a story they thought may help. It was the story Jesus told of a little old widow who was finding it difficult to get justice from a big crooked judge. She finally got justice by knocking on his door at all hours of the night for week after week.

As we discussed the story with them, hope began to rise out of their hopelessness. As hope was born, so was a new sense of power. They started discussing the possible solutions in a whole new light. They decided to take up a petition to present to the city council and to persist until they got a fair hearing.

They gathered hundreds of signatures and organised a march to the city council administration centre to present the petitions. Then they followed up on the people who could change the decision. Finally, through perseverance they had learned about in the story of the little old widow and the big crooked judge, they were granted an alternative place to stay where the community would have their own houses on their own land. Not only that, the council would help pay the expenses of their move.

It was more than they had ever dreamed possible. The move also opened up a whole host of new doors. Not only did they now have their own homes on their own land, they could now develop their own education, health and employment programmes. This whole group, numbering hundreds, now started to experience good changes in their style of life.

With the decrease in demoralisation came an increase in morality in the community. There was a marked decrease in domestic violence and child abuse. Constructive work increased and people engaged in more fulfilling recreation. There were more harmonious couples and healthier children. Fewer people went to untimely graves. Not only did they live longer, they also lived fuller lives.

And at the centre of all this change was a group in the community who had not forgotten that the personal growth and social change had come because they had followed the agenda of God, personified in Jesus. This group were just not content with the changes in the past. They also looked into the future and saw the changes that were possible if they followed in the footsteps of Jesus of Nazareth and like him, lived in sympathy with the heart of God.

How can we facilitate transformation of a community that is not self-destructive or self-defeating?
By ensuring that personal growth and social change are in sympathy with God's agenda for the world as personified in the life of Jesus and exemplified in the prophetic tradition.

IDEAS FOR MEDITATION, DISCUSSION AND ACTION

1. **Reflect**: What are we trying to accomplish in our community?
2. **Relate**: How crucial is conversion to the authentic personal growth and social change for which we strive?
3. **Respond**: What will you do to help bring about prophetic transformation in your community?

EPILOGUE

STRAIGHT FROM THE HEART

The sayings of Jesus and the stories of Jesus confront us with truth straight from the heart of God. Nothing challenges our opinions and prejudices or calls us to a cause of pure compassion more than these sayings and stories.

The following two sections are not a theoretical look at these sayings and stories, but a practical introduction to the way these sayings and stories can help us change ourselves and change our world.

SAYINGS OF THE HEART

The sayings of Jesus are simple and practical; simple enough to understand, practical enough for anyone to put them into practice.

To mouth the sayings of Jesus is religious – but to act on them is revolutionary.

Whenever the sayings are not translated into action they are reduced to meaningless clichés; a religious rhetoric about unrealised ideals that are worse than useless in a world which is sick and tired of a piety that refuses to roll its sleeves up and lend a hand to those in need.

However, when the sayings of Jesus are translated into action, the ideals become ideas that work; a divine agenda for radical yet viable personal growth and social change which enables us to work towards the realisation of our dreams for a better world.

We can translate these sayings into action by following these steps:

1. Select a saying that speaks to our situation. 'Which of Jesus's sayings is relevant to my situation?'

2. Meditate on that saying. 'What does Jesus's saying tell me about how he would approach my situation?' Ask the question and listen carefully, imaginatively and creatively for the answer.

3. Translate the saying into action. 'How could I approach my situation in the way Jesus would?' Experiment with the truth. Practice the love and justice which are the heart of the saying.

4. Reflect on the translation. 'Did I really take the heart of the saying to heart?' Evaluate the experiment with truth and try again. Practice makes perfect.

Here are just a few of the sayings of Jesus for us to begin translating into action.

SAYINGS ABOUT TRUTH, LOVE AND JUSTICE

There is only one who is good. God.
You must be as good as God.

Matthew 19:17 & Luke 18:19

Unless your quest for justice gets beyond that of religious people, you can't even start to be involved in God's movement.

Matthew 5:20

Beware of the experts . . .

Luke 20:46

Why don't you judge for yourself what is right?

Luke 12:57

Stop judging people by mere appearances and make right judgments.

John 7:24

What the world esteems is disgusting to God.

Luke 16:15

Everyone who exalts himself
　　will be humbled.
Everyone who humbles himself
　　will be exalted.

Luke 18:14

Those who are last,
　　will be first.
Those who are first,
　　will be last.

Luke 13:30

How sad it is for you who neglect to do justice.

Luke 11:42

How sad it is for you who load people down with burdens
they cannot bear and you yourselves will not even lift a
finger to help.

Luke 11:46

How sad it is for the world
　　because of the things
　　　　that cause people to sin.

Matthew 18:7

The temptation to do wrong is inevitable,
but how sad it is for you who do the tempting.

Matthew 18:7

How sad it is for you who are rich for you have already
received your comfort.

Luke 6:24

How happy are the poor in spirit, for God's movement is
for them.

Matthew 5:3

How sad it is for you that are well fed now, for you will go
hungry.

Luke 6:25

How happy are you that hunger now for you will be satisfied.

Luke 6:21

How sad it is for you who laugh now for you will weep . . .

Luke 6:25

How happy are those who weep now for you will laugh.

Luke 6:21

How sad it is for you when all men speak well of you, for that is how their fathers treated false prophets.

Luke 6:26

How happy are you when men hate you and insult you . . . and exclude you, because you follow the True Leader.

Luke 6:22

How happy are the pure in heart for they will see God.

Matthew 5:8

How happy are the peacemakers for they will be known as the children of God.

Matthew 5:9

How happy are those who cry for they will be comforted.

Matthew 5:4

How happy are those who show mercy for they will be shown mercy.

Matthew 5:7

How happy are those who hunger and thirst for justice for they will be satisfied.

Matthew 5:6

How happy are those who are persecuted because of their commitment to the cause of justice, for God's movement is for them.

Matthew 5:10

How happy are those who manage their affairs justly for they will have the earth as their heritage.

Matthew 5:5

A woman giving birth to a child has pain. But when the baby is born she forgets the anguish because of her joy that a child is born into the world.

John 16:21

You will cry . . . while the world rejoices . . . But your grief will turn to joy.

John 16:20

You will rejoice, and no one will take away your joy.

John 16:22

Happy are those who believe without seeing.

John 20:29

Happy are those who hear the word of God and obey it.

Luke 11:28

Be careful, or your hearts will be overwhelmed by self-indulgence, drunkenness . . . and distractions in life.

Luke 12:15

Never be troubled about tomorrow,
    tomorrow can take care of itself.
Today's troubles are enough
    for today.

Matthew 6:34

Who of you by worrying
    can add a single hour to his life?
Since you cannot do this very simple thing,
    why do you worry about the rest?

Luke 12:25–26

Do not be anxious about your life,
    about what you can get to eat or drink.
Is not life more important
    than its nourishment?

Matthew 6:25

What good will it do if someone gains the whole world and loses his soul?

Matthew 16:26

Unless a person starts life all over again,
   they cannot be a part of God's movement.

John 3:3

Set your heart on God's movement and his justice.

Matthew 6:33

Those who do justice will shine like the sun.

Matthew 13:43

You are the light of the world.

Matthew 5:14

Let your light so shine that people may see the good you do
and praise your Father who is in heaven.

Matthew 5:16

SAYINGS ABOUT SIMPLICITY, SOLIDARITY AND SERVICE

Love the Lord your God
with all your heart
with all your soul
with all your strength
and with all your mind.

Luke 10:27

Give to the government what belongs to the government
and to God, what belongs to God.

Matthew 22:21

You must serve God or money.
You cannot serve both.

Matthew 6:24

Be on guard against all kinds of greed.

Luke 12:15

Give to anyone who asks for anything.
If anyone wants to borrow anything . . . let him have it.

Matthew 5:42

Lend . . . without expecting anything back.

Luke 6:35

If anyone takes what belongs to you, do not demand it back.

Luke 6:30

Sell everything and give to the poor.

Luke 18:22

SAYINGS ABOUT COMPASSION, ACCEPTANCE AND RESPECT

God is compassionate
  even to people who don't appreciate it.
Be compassionate
  even as your Father in heaven is compassionate.

Luke 6:35–36

Don't make a show of your religion
  in order to attract attention to yourself.

Matthew 6:1

Whenever you do someone a favour,
  don't tell the world about it.

Matthew 6:3

Always treat other people as you would like them to treat you.

Matthew 7:12

Whoever wants to be a leader must be willing to be a servant.

Matthew 20:26

When someone invites you to a special function,
  do not take a place of honour.

Luke 14:8

When you give a luncheon
  do not invite your friends . . .
                or relatives . . .
                or affluent neighbours.
But when you give a banquet
  invite the destitute . . .
        the disabled . . .
        the blind.

Luke 14:12–13

Treat older people with respect.

Luke 18:20

Do not treat children with contempt.

Matthew 18:10

Love your neighbour as yourself.

Luke 10:27

SAYINGS ABOUT CONFLICT, CONFRONTATION AND SUFFERING

In the world you will have trouble.

John 16:33

Don't put your trust in people.

Matthew 10:17

A good tree always yields good fruit,
and a bad tree always yields bad fruit . . .
By their fruits you will know them.

Matthew 7:17, 20

Be shrewd . . .
  but be harmless . . .

Matthew 10:16

Don't react to anyone who wants to harm you.

Matthew 5:39

Do good to those who would do evil to you.
Love those who hate you.
Bless those who curse you.

Matthew 5:44

If anyone hits you on one cheek,
   turn the other cheek.

Matthew 5:39

Begin by getting the plank out of your own eye, before taking the speck out of someone else's.

Matthew 7:3

If your brother does something wrong, take him to task.
If he is sorry, forgive him.
If he does you wrong seven times a day,
   and seven times a day comes back to you
   and says he is sorry,
forgive him.

Luke 17:3–4

If a brother wrongs you, go and show him his fault between him and you alone. If he listens to you, you have got your brother back.
But if he will not listen to you, take one or two others with you, that every word may be confirmed on the evidence of two or three witnesses.
If he refuses to listen to them, tell it to the community. If he pays no attention to the community, you just have to treat him like anybody else.

Matthew 18:17

Let the dead bury the dead.

Matthew 8:22

Don't be afraid of those who can kill the body but not the soul.

Matthew 10:28

SAYINGS ABOUT POWER, POSSIBILITY AND RESPONSIBILITY

With God anything is possible.

                                        Matthew 19:26

Don't make a move until you have been infused with power from on high.

                                        Luke 24:49

Nothing shall be impossible to you.

                                        Matthew 17:20

Follow me.

                                        Matthew 8:22

If anyone wishes to follow in my footsteps,
   he must disregard himself,
   be ready to die,
and follow me.

                                        Matthew 16:24

He who is concerned about gaining his life will lose it,
But by losing his life for my sake, he will gain it.

                                        Matthew 10:39

God's movement is here and now in you.

                                        Luke 17:21

Don't tell anyone,
   but show them,
      and let them see for themselves.

                                        Luke 5:14

Cure the sick. Raise the dead.

                                        Matthew 10:8

As long as it is day we must work.
Night is coming when no one can work.

                                        John 9:4

STORIES FOR THE HEART

The stories Jesus told, and the stories told about Jesus, can be an invaluable resource for those who want to be involved in meeting community needs. Like a road map for a traveller exploring unfamiliar territory, they give us direction.

I once suggested to my father, a preacher of note who teaches potential preachers how to preach, that the best thing he could do for the community was proclaim a moratorium on preaching. He was horrified but kindly asked me to explain.

I told him I thought the time could be used better by getting the large congregation to break up into small groups to study the stories of Jesus and seek to live out the storylines in their own lives.

I am convinced that it is only as we allow the stories of Jesus to reframe our involvement in the community that we will be able to practise what we preach.

My father never did proclaim a moratorium on preaching, but both of us have done our best to help groups of people study the stories of Jesus. Both of us are convinced that we must treat these stories as road maps to be followed rather than picture postcards to be admired. If we follow the directions laid out in these stories, we will find ourselves inevitably following the footsteps of Jesus into the struggle for love and justice in our community.

I have developed some studies of the stories of Jesus that have been helpful to groups I have worked with. While they are designed primarily for small groups, individuals can also use them. Here are some simple guidelines to get the most out of these studies.

1. Begin with prayer.
2. The questions to be answered in the study should be read aloud by the study leader.
3. Trust the questions.
4. Listen to the answers. Take your time.
5. Discourage any one person from dominating.
6. Encourage people not to debate with each other but to understand one another.
7. Avoid sidetracks by suggesting side issues be discussed over coffee later.
8. When there is difficulty answering the questions, acknowledge the difficulty but don't give up trying to answer the questions.
9. End with the exercise suggested.

STUDY 1:   THE SPIRIT OF JESUS

1. What purpose do we believe God has for us?
2. Read about the purpose Jesus believed the Spirit of God had for him.

> Jesus came to Nazareth, the little town where he had been brought up, on a Sunday and went to church like he always did.
>
> An attendant asked him to share something from the Old Book. So he read the manifesto, written by a prophet called Isaiah, for the long awaited leader.
>
> 'The Spirit of God has got hold of me,
> and is urging me to do a special job;
> share good news with the poor;
> free the prisoners;
> help the handicapped;
> and smash the shackles of the oppressed.'
>
> Then he closed the book, handed it back to the attendant, and sat down.
>
> Well, you could have heard a pin drop.

The whole church stared at him. So he looked around at them all and said, 'Today this announcement has come true. I have made this manifesto my own!'

(Luke 4:16–21, adapted)

3. Compare this sense of purpose with ours.

    * What are the similarities?
    * What are the differences?
    * Why?

4. How do we think Jesus understood the Nazareth Manifesto? What kind of involvement with people did it mean for Jesus?
5. Who are the poor in our world today?
6. What would be good news for these people?
7. Who are those in prison in our world?
8. How can we work for their release?
9. Who are those with handicaps in our world?
10. How can we enable those with disabilities function more fully and more effectively in our society?
11. Who are the oppressed in our society?
12. How can we work to break the shackles of the oppressed?
13. What did Jesus indicate was the source of the power for the struggle for justice?
14. How is this kind of power different from other kinds of power?
15. How can we derive strength from the power of the Spirit?

Exercise: Let's reconsider the purpose we believe God has for us after meditating on the Nazareth Manifesto.

Let's open our hearts to the Spirit of God and write a manifesto for our own lives.

Now let's share our manifesto with others.

Spend a few minutes in silence thinking about what these manifestos may mean to the way we live our lives as individuals and as a group.

Talk about the implications of these manifestos with one another over coffee.

STUDY 2:   THE PRINCIPLE OF JUSTICE

1. Define justice and describe an incident that illustrates
our idea of justice.
2. Read the following story told by Jesus:

> At the end of time, Jesus said, the True Leader will
> gather everyone together for the final reckoning. Like a
> stockman culling wild horses, the True Leader will di-
> vide those gathered into two groups. Those who have
> done the right thing will be put on his right and those who
> haven't on his left.

> To those on his right, the True Leader issues an invi-
> tation to a never-ending party. 'Come!' he says. 'For I
> was hungry as a horse and you gave me a feed. I was as
> dry as a parched gully and you gave me a drink. I just
> arrived in town and you took me into your home. My
> clothes were in tatters and you gave me a great outfit. I
> was sick in bed and you came and spent time with me. I
> was stuck in jail and you stuck by me and my family.'

> The people on the right were stumped. 'When on earth
> did we see you hungry and give you a feed or thirsty and
> give you a drink?' they queried. 'When did we meet you
> after you had just arrived in town and give you a bed for
> the night? When were you sick in bed and we visited
> you? When were you stuck in jail and we looked after
> you and your family?'

> The True Leader replied, 'Whenever you did the right
> thing by those who most people wouldn't give a damn
> for, you did the right thing by me.'

> Then turning to those on his left the True Leader says,
> 'Get out. You're in big trouble! You can go to hell with
> all those who made life a misery for others. I was hungry
> and you never gave me a feed, thirsty and you never gave
> me a drink, lonely without a friend and you walked by,
> half-naked and you didn't give me clothes, sick in bed
> and stuck in jail and you didn't even visit.'

Those on the left were bewildered. 'When did we see you hungry or thirsty?' they cried. 'When did we see you lonely without a friend or half-naked and badly in need of a new set of clothes? When did we see you sick in bed or stuck in jail?'

The True Leader replied, 'Whenever you ignored the needs of those whom most people consider least, you ignored me.' (Matthew 25:31–46, adapted)

3. Both groups of people in the above story were surprised at the connection Jesus made between the way they had treated those whom most consider least and the True Leader. Why?

4. Other parts of the Scriptures also stress God's relationship with the poor. e.g. Proverbs 14:31. What are our reactions to Jesus stressing this relationship by saying we will be judged on Judgment Day by the way we have treated the poor?

5. What is the measure by which we will all be judged?

6. Who are those 'that most consider least' in our society?

7. How can we change the way we treat those 'that most consider least' so that we begin to do them justice?

8. In what ways are we most likely not to do the right thing by those 'that most consider least'?

9. What excuses do we usually use to rationalise our failures?

10. What do we imagine God's response will be to our rationalisations at the time of reckoning?

11. How can we make sure we succeed more often in doing the right thing by those 'that most consider least'?

Exercise: Spend some time thinking about a specific choice we are faced with at the moment.

Who do we normally discount in making such a choice?

How could we make this choice so as to do justice to those we usually don't take into account?

Share with the group the choice we have to make and how we are going to resolve it.

STUDY 3:   THE LIGHT IN THE DARKNESS
                MISSION

1. Turn off the lights or darken the room and discuss the
question: How does being in darkness make us feel?
2. Light a candle. How does it affect us when we are
trapped in darkness and someone lights a candle?
3. Read the following statement by Jesus:

> 'You are the world's light.
> It is impossible to hide a town built on the top of a hill.
> Have you ever heard of anyone lighting a candle and
> putting it under the table?
> Don't you put it on a candlestick on the table so it gives
> light to everyone in the room?
> Well then, since you are the world's light, go ahead and
> shine so brightly that when people see the good things
> you do they'll thank God.'

(Matthew 5:14–16, adapted)

4. What is the nature of the darkness in us and around us?
5. Who are the light of the world?
6. Why does Jesus insist we can be the light of the world?
7. How does that make us feel?
8. Why do we think Jesus used the image of a candle rather
than something like lightning?
9. When we think of what we have to offer the world, what
do we think would describe it best; a candle, a sixty-watt
light bulb or a flood light?
10. In Jesus's statement, he says that our light is 'the good
things we do'. Why do we think Jesus said that the light the
world needs is not good intentions, not good words, but
good deeds?
11. Think of the good things others have done in our
community. Which of these do we think effectively confronted the darkness and infused light into our community?
12. What would make us want to hide our candle under the
table?

Exercise: Think of one 'good thing' we could do in our neighbourhood that people would thank God for. Decide when and how we will do that 'good thing'. Let's share our decision with the group.

Think of the excuses we have used to hide our candle under the table. Let's ask God for his help to help us put our candle in a place where it will bring the most light.

STUDY 4: THE YEAST IN THE FLOUR MOVEMENT

1. Have someone who has made bread tell us how they made it.
2. Read the following short statement:

Jesus told them another illustration.
'The God movement is like yeast which a woman took and mixed into a large amount of flour until the whole had risen.'

(Matthew 13:33, adapted)

3. Why did Jesus use this image to illustrate the way God's movement develops on earth?
4. If we used this image as a model for the role of believers in their neighbourhood, who would we identify as the yeast and who would we identify as the flour? Why?
5. What does the yeast have to offer to the flour?
6. What can we offer to our neighbourhood?
7. What does the flour have to offer the yeast?
8. What can our neighbourhood offer to us?
9. How must the yeast and the flour be combined if the bread is to rise properly?
10. How can we, as believers, be as well integrated into our neighbourhood as that?
11. Why does Jesus insist that the significance of the yeast is not in the difference between the yeast and the flour, but

in the difference the yeast makes with the flour to the combined mixture?

12. What difference do we make to our community?

13. According to this illustration, what is the most effective way in which believers could make a difference in our neighbourhoods?

Exercise: Think of one way we can become yeast in our neighbourhoods.

Decide when and how we can do it.

Let's break into pairs, share our decision with our partner and make arrangements to contact each other within seven days to see how we are going with implementing our decision.

STUDY 5: THE WAITERS' ASSOCIATION

1. When organisations have a job to do, how do they usually organise those employed to do the job?

2. Why do we think the structure of bosses and workers is so universally accepted?

3. Read what Jesus has to say about bosses:

> We all know that bosses call the shots and heavies throw their weight around.
> But that's not the way you should do things.
> If you want to be a leader . . . don't be a boss. Let others call the shots . . . and do the work yourself.
> For the True Leader didn't come to be waited on, but to be a waiter . . . spending the whole of his life so that others could have a life worth living.
>
> (Matthew 20:25–28, adapted)

4. What does Jesus say about the usual way we organise workers to get the job done?

5. What is his alternative way of getting the job done?

6. How do we imagine adopting this alternative would work out in practice?

7. What are the similarities and differences between the traditional style of leadership and Jesus's alternative?

8. What are the strengths and weaknesses of the traditional style?

9. What are the strengths and weaknesses of Jesus's alternative?

10. What style of leader would we prefer to work with? Why?

11. Why do we think Jesus insisted on our being workers rather than bosses?

Exercise: Let's think of ways we can be waiters in our family, the market place, the workplace, the church and the locality.

Let's talk it over with each other and make ourselves accountable to each other for the efforts we will make to be waiters in our community.

STUDY 6: THE RADICAL AGENDA

1. Read the following story that shows the radical agenda Jesus set for people:

A man came up to Jesus and put it to him, 'Teacher, what do I need to do to be okay from here on out?'

Jesus said, 'Why ask me? . . . If you want to live life as you ought to, just obey the rules for living.'

'What rules?' the man enquired.

Jesus replied, 'Don't murder. Don't screw around. Don't steal and don't lie. Look after the old folks and look out for your neighbour's interests like you'd look out for your own.'

'Gee, I've done all that,' the man replied. 'What more do I need to do?'

Jesus replied, 'If you really want to get your act together, go and sell your property and give all the proceeds to the poor . . . and come follow me.'

When the young man heard what Jesus said, he turned away in terrible distress because he had a lot of property and didn't want to part with it.

Then Jesus said to his followers, 'It is extremely difficult for the affluent to be a part of the movement. In fact, it's easier to get a fully loaded semi-trailer through the keyhole of a housing commission house than it is to get a wealthy person to be a part of God's movement among the poor.'

When the followers of Jesus heard this, they freaked out. 'Who of us can make it then?'

'Humanly speaking,' Jesus said, 'it is impossible. But with God anything is possible.'

Peter said, 'We've left everything to follow you. What's in it for us?'

Jesus reassured him, 'When the True Leader comes into his own path with all his supporters, you will have an important part in the administration.

'Everyone who has given up property or relationships for the sake of my cause will go through a tough time, but they will get more than enough to meet their needs . . .

'Just remember. Many who are first now will be last then, and many who are last now will be first then!'

(Matthew 19:16–30, adapted)

2. What was the man's question?
3. How would we have answered him?
4. When the man claimed to be good, Jesus did not counter his claim. Instead, he pointed out that he was not good enough. What was required of him to be truly good?
5. Why do we imagine Jesus answered him this way? Why was it necessary for him to give his wealth to the poor for him to be truly good?
6. Do we think the reason Jesus considered this rich young aristocrat was sinning by hanging on to his wealth was:
    (a) money had become his god.
    (b) he was omitting to take action that could redress injustice.
    (c) both of the above.
    (d) none of the above.
7. If Jesus told us that for us to be truly good we must

follow this same radical agenda, how would we react?

8. Do we consider that we are rich?

9. Riches are relative. How do we normally measure whether we are rich or not?

10. Compared to the poverty of the majority of the world's population, do we think Jesus would look at us as affluent or poor? How does this make us feel?

11. Why do we think Jesus said it is so hard that it is humanly impossible for the affluent to give up their riches and share them with the poor?

12. Why do we think Jesus stuck to his guns over the radical demands of his agenda instead of making it easier by demanding less?

13. In what ways do we try to moderate the radical demands that Jesus makes on us through this story?

14. How do we imagine that God might be able to enable us to follow this radical agenda of Jesus?

15. What security did Jesus offer to those who risked all to take his radical agenda seriously?

16. Do we know of anyone who has taken this radical agenda to heart? Let's share their story with the group.

Exercise: Let's close our eyes and imagine Jesus standing in front of us, telling us to abandon our affluence and follow him.

Let's recognise that humanly speaking it is impossible for us to obey but ask God for his help to follow his command.

Let's choose one way that we can put the last first this week and share our resources with those who need them more than us.

Let's not tell everyone, but let's tell one person what we have decided to do and report back to them when we have done what we have said we will do.

STUDY 7:   THE REVOLUTIONARY PROGRAMME

1. Read the following revolutionary principles Jesus spelled out to people:

Love those who hate you and be kind to those who would like to kill you.

Bless those who curse you and pray for those who put you down.

Even if they beat you up, embrace them.

Even if they rip you off, help them out.

If someone needs something, give it to them. Don't try to get back anything they take.

Treat others as you would like them to treat you.

(Luke 6:27–31, adapted)

2. What is the difference between the way we usually act and the way Jesus suggests we ought to act?

3. How do we feel about Jesus's programme? Why?

4. What difference do we think it would make to our world if people followed this programme? Why?

5. What human principle is the programme based on?

6. Do we think we treat this principle as a cliché or do we use it as a basis for the way we relate to others?

7. What are some common circumstances where we could put this programme into operation and what effect do we think it would have?

8. Read the following further revolutionary principles Jesus spelled out to people:

If you love those who love you . . . big deal! Everybody does that.

If you do good to those who do good to you . . . where's the grace in that? Everybody acts that way already.

If you give with the expectation of getting something back . . . you're just doing business as usual.

Love those who hate you.

Do good to those who are bad to you.

Give yourself fully and freely without any expectations of getting anything back.

Then you'll have something to be really pleased about.

Your actions will reflect the character of God.

(Luke 6:32–36, adapted)

9. Why does Jesus dismiss our love, the good we do and the giving of ourselves as being of no real significance?

10. What does Jesus suggest will be the only way we can make a significant difference to our society?

11. What is the divine principle on which the programme is based?

12. Why is this principle so revolutionary?

Exercise: Think of someone who is giving us a hard time. Let's pray for them, asking God to bless them. Now let's decide how we will return good for evil.

STUDY 8:   THE BLOODY STRUGGLE

1. Read about the bloody struggle to which Jesus calls us:

> Do not imagine that I have come to bring tranquillity. I have not come to bring a gin and tonic, but a gun. For I have come to put people in conflict with each other . . . even in their own family.
> Anyone who cares more for their parents than they care for me and my cause doesn't deserve to be a part of the movement.
> Anyone who cares more for their children than they care for me and my cause doesn't deserve to be part of the movement.
> Anyone who wants to follow in my footsteps but is not willing to face the firing squad is not good enough for me.
> Anyone who tries to preserve their life will waste it, but anyone who wastes their life for me and my movement will preserve the spirit that makes life worth living.
>
> (Matthew 10:34–39, adapted)

2. What does the gun stand for?

3. How do we react to the statement that Jesus has 'not come to bring a gin and tonic but a gun?'

4. What kind of conflict does Jesus say the struggle will involve?

5. How do we feel about such conflicts even if they are for the sake of a good cause? Why?

6. Elsewhere Jesus says we must take care of our families

so what does he mean when he says that anyone who cares more for their parents or their children than they care for him or his cause doesn't deserve to be a part of the movement?

7. What does the firing squad stand for?

8. In the conflict Jesus envisaged, he talks about bringing a gun but not using a gun; facing a firing squad not being a firing squad; dying rather than killing. What does this tell us about the conduct he expects from those involved in the struggle for love and justice?

9. Why can we expect that those who struggle for love and justice will face conflict and suffering?

10. What are some contemporary examples of those who have set aside security, safety and comfort to become involved in the bloody struggle for love and justice and ultimately 'faced the firing squad'?

11. In what ways are they models for the way we should follow Jesus in the ongoing struggle?

12. Are we willing to join them in the ongoing struggle?

13. What may be the consequences if we do?

14. What are the consequences of not getting involved?

15. What do we think Jesus meant when he concluded by saying, 'Anyone who tries to preserve their life will waste it, but anyone who wastes their life for me and my movement will preserve the spirit that makes life worth living'?

Exercise: Think of an issue of love and justice, where, if we stood up and were counted, conflict would be created. Let's share this with the rest of the group and then allow the group to pray for us, asking God to give us the courage to face that conflict.

Over coffee, let's discuss how, as a group, we may be able to stand with each other and encourage each other to take steps to work for love and justice in the face of possible violence.

STUDY 9: THE MUSTARD SEED CONSPIRACY

1. What do we think we can achieve in terms of real change in our society?

2. How do we feel when we seem to be so small compared to the big forces that we are up against?

3. Read the following short statements about the mustard seed conspiracy:

> Listen . . . the mustard seed is the smallest seed of them all, yet when it grows it is the biggest tree in the garden. Its branches become a haven for wild birds to build their nest.
>
> (Matthew 13:31, adapted)

4. Why do we think Jesus uses a tiny seed to symbolise our efforts?

5. Why doesn't Jesus consider small efforts insignificant?

6. What reasons do we have for believing that the 'smallest' effort might in the long run be of the 'greatest' significance?

7. What can we do to encourage one another to live as if the 'smallest' efforts can be of the 'greatest' significance?

8. What examples do we know of people whose efforts appeared to have very little significance, yet in the end, these efforts turned out to be of great significance to society?

9. What does the picture of a tiny seed becoming a tree where wild birds build their nest convey to us?

10. How can we use this imagery of trees and nests to evaluate the effectiveness of our efforts?

11. What has to happen to the seed before it becomes this tree?

Exercise: Think of one way we can bury ourselves in the lives of others.

Let's share our decision with someone else.

Let's pray that our mustard seed effort may blossom into a tree of refuge for those in trouble.

Then let's discuss how together we can create alternative structures for the protection and support of people in trouble in our locality.

SUGGESTIONS FOR STUDY

I would recommend a range of literature which might be as valuable to you as it has been for me in developing a spirituality for a servant church in contemporary society.

Many of us are uncertain how to cultivate a spiritual life which is vital and relevant. In *Celebration of Discipline* (Hodder & Stoughton, 1981), Richard Foster shows how the classical disciplines of meditation, prayer, study, simplicity, solitude, submission, service, confession, worship, guidance and celebration can continue to promote the courage and joy to engage our world which we need today.

In *Freedom of Simplicity* (SPCK, 1981), Richard Foster indicates how simplicity can be developed in a materialistic society by making God's movement for love and justice a priority in all aspects of our lives. In *Money, Sex and Power* (Hodder & Stoughton, 1985), Richard Foster illustrates how we can respond to the dominant and determining issues in modern society authentically and creatively.

The Upside Down Kingdom (Marshall, Morgan and Scott, 1985) by Donald B. Kraybill is a study of the words and deeds of Jesus of Nazareth which provide practical ways to engage and change our world.

The Mustard Seed Conspiracy (MARC Europe, 1985) by Tom Sire is an analysis of our current global situation and the latest models of church involvement in the community, both in the first world, and in the two third worlds.

In *Paul's Idea of Community* (Paternoster Press, 1981), Robert Banks presents a theological interpretation of community, looking at the early house churches in their historical setting.

In *The Home Church* (Albatross) Robert and Julia Banks translate the meaning of their theological interpretation of community into the way in which we can live out the mission of the church in our own home in our own area.

In *Community and Growth* (Darton, Longman and Todd, 1979), Jean Vanier shares some of the wisdom that he has gained from living with lonely people about the meaning of cultivating a common life in which people can change and grow.

In *Being There for Others* (The Joint Board of Christian Education), Bruce Turley offers steps towards caring for people in our community, and *Expanding Horizons of Care* by the same author (The Joint Board of Christian Education) helps us to discern how we can take a stand on issues that affect the people we care for in our community.

The Church and Community Development by George Lovell (Grail Publications, 1972) is an excellent account of practical methods that the church can use in its work in the community. *Human and Religious Factors in Church and Community Work* (Grail Publications, 1982), also by George Lovell, is an honest evaluation of the strengths and weaknesses of the practical methods that the church can use in its work in the community.